W9-AAS-444

FooLISH

WORDS

BY LAURA WARD

This company is not bust. We are merely in a cyclical decline.
Lord Stokes, on British Leyland

I would like to thank my parents—especially my father and mother.
Golfer, Greg Norman

The problem with the French is that they don't have a word for entrepreneur.
George W. Bush

I just want to thank everyone I met in my entire life.
Kim Basinger's Oscar acceptance speech

China is a big country, inhabited by many Chinese.
Charles de Gaulle

So where's the Cannes film festival being held this year?
Christina Aguilera

To have your niece die in your arms is the greatest gift from God.
Celine Dion

I believe there would be people alive today if there were a death penalty.
Nancy Reagan

FOOLISH WORDS

WORDS

BY LAURA WARD

The Most Stupid Words Ever Spoken

STERLING

New York / London
www.sterlingpublishing.com

STERLING and the distinctive Sterling logo are registered trademarks of Sterling Publishing Co., Inc.

10 9 8 7 6 5 4 3 2 1

Published by Sterling Publishing Co., Inc.
387 Park Avenue South, New York, NY 10016
© 2009 Anova Book Company Limited
Distributed in Canada by Sterling Publishing
c/o Canadian Manda Group, 165 Dufferin Street
Toronto, Ontario, Canada M6K 3H6
Distributed in the United Kingdom by GMC
Distribution Services
Castle Place, 166 High Street, Lewes, East Sussex,
England BN7 1XU
Distributed in Australia by Capricorn Link
(Australia) Pty. Ltd.
P.O. Box 704, Windsor, NSW 2756, Australia

Printed by NPE Print Communications Pte Ltd, Singapore
All rights reserved

Sterling ISBN 978-1-4027-6830-9

For information about custom editions, special sales,
premium and corporate purchases, please contact
Sterling Special Sales
Department at 800-805-5489 or
specialsales@sterlingpublishing.com.

CONTENTS:

BRAIN in NEUTRAL — MOUTH in DRIVE

One thing I can't understand is why the newspapers labeled me **"The Mad Bomber."** That was unkind.

George Matesky, on his arrest for placing 20 bombs in public places over a 17-year period, New York, *Journal-American*, January 22, 1957

Princess Anne

We've never had a holiday. A week or two at Balmoral, or ten days at Sandringham is the nearest we get.

The people in the Navy look on motherhood as being compatible with being a woman.

Rear Admiral James R. Hogg

Interviewer: "Have you ever thought of writing your autobiography?"
Boxer Chris Eubank: "On what?"

Suddenly, I was subjected to a particularly nasty, totally unexpected and unprovoked attack.

Serial killer Peter Sutcliffe, aka "The Yorkshire Ripper," on how he was assaulted by a fellow inmate

Many people never stop to realize that a tree is a living thing, not that different from a tall, leafy dog that has roots and is very quiet.
Jack Handey, environmentalist

He [Chris Coleman] swerved to avoid what he thinks was a deer. It all happened so fast. He also said the animal could have been something smaller, like a rabbit.
Friend of Fulham soccer player Chris Coleman describing the accident that all but ended Coleman's playing career

Alan Brazil: "I was sad to hear yesterday about the death of Inspector Morse, John Shaw."
TalkSport Co-Host: "John Thaw, Alan."
Alan Brazil: "Do you know, I've been doing that all morning. John, if you're listening, sorry, mate."
Exchange on TalkSport radio

We don't necessarily **discriminate**. We simply **exclude** certain types of people.
Colonel Gerald Wellman, Reserve Officer Training Corps

The best thing to do with a degree is to forget it.
Prince Philip, at the University of Salford

Would you, my dear young friends, like to be inside with the **five wise virgins**, or outside, alone and in the dark with the foolish ones?
Montagu Butler, preaching to a congregation of undergraduates at Trinity Chapel, Cambridge

I thought my window was down, but I found out it was up when I put my head through it.
Detail of the circumstances of an accident in a claim submitted to an insurance company

Major General Charles F. Kuyk Jr.

The Air Force is pleased with the performance of the C-5A cargo plane, although having the wings fall off at eight thousand feet is a problem.

Had Christ died in my van, with people around him who loved him . . . (his death) would have been far more dignified.
Dr. Jack Kevorkian, physician and euthanasia activist, USA Today, July 30, 1996

The bride is on the right.
TV commentator, stating the obvious as Lady Diana Spencer set off down the aisle on her father's arm on her wedding day, 1981

Life is indeed precious. And I believe the death penalty helps to affirm this fact.

Ed Koch, Mayor of New York City

WeightWatchers will meet at 7pm at the First Presbyterian Church. Please use the large, double door at the side entrance.
Church bulletin

And now the sequence of events, in no particular order.
Dan Rather, TV anchorman, during a radio broadcast

If everyone on earth just stopped breathing for an hour, the greenhouse effect would no longer be a problem.
Jerry Adler, *Newsweek*, December 31, 1990

All those magnificent balls on deck.

Retired Royal Navy officer Captain Sam Lombard-Hobson, wistfully recalling the days when smart dances were still held aboard ship, on BBC Radio 4's Today program, June 1983

In Oxford, a jury has been told that Donald Neilson denied he was the Pink Panther.
BBC Radio 4 newscaster Edward Cole reading a headline about an alleged murderer dubbed "The Black Panther" by the press

At the present moment, the whole Fleet is lit up. When I say "lit up," I mean lit up by fairy lamps. We've forgotten the whole Royal Review . . . The whole thing is lit up by fairy lamps. It's fantastic. It isn't the Fleet at all. It's just . . . it's just fairy land. The whole Fleet is in fairy land . . .
Lieutenant-Commander Tommy Woodrooffe, a leading BBC radio commentator of the 1930s, during what was to have been a 15-minute commentary of the "illumination" of the British Fleet on the night of the Coronation Naval Review at Spithead. (He was faded out after less than four minutes.)

Sean Rafferty, Radio 3

And that was played by the Lindsay String Quartet . . . or at least two-thirds of them.

An invisible car came out of nowhere, struck my car and vanished.

Detail of an accident in a claim submitted to an insurance company

The weather will be cold. There are two reasons for this. One is that the temperatures will be lower.
Radio weather forecast, April 12, 1969

An end is in sight to the severe weather shortage.

Ian Macaskill, optimistic weatherman

John Snow: "In a sense, Deng Xiaoping's death was inevitable, wasn't it?"
Expert: "Er, yes."
Channel 4 News

Do you believe David Trimble will stick to his guns on decommissioning?
Interviewer, Ulster TV

In life he was a living legend; in death, nothing has changed.
Live TV

The Chancellor of the Exchequer has just begun to announce his bunny midget.
James Alexander Gordon, BBC Radio 2 announcer, with a newsflash on the forthcoming mini-budget

Ah, the Queen has just left the bridge of HMS *Vanguard* and has gone down below for some reason or other . . . (interminable pause) . . . and now I can see water coming through the side of the ship . . .
John Snagge, trying hard to spin out his commentary during the visit of the King and Queen (George VI and Elizabeth) to Canada in 1939

Has anyone here been raped and speaks English?

Crass TV reporter in the Congo in 1960, among a crowd of Belgian civilians during the war of independence. The phrase became the title of a book by Edward Behr in 1978

Israeli troops have this morning entered the Arab township of Hebron, in search of the perpetrators of the recent suicide bomb attacks.
CNN News

I was on my way to the doctor with rear end trouble when my universal joint gave way, causing me to have an accident.
Detail of the "accident in question" in a claim submitted to an insurance company

"Analysis" by Linda Ellerbee, CNN PrimeNews, June 2 , 1989

"These boat people," says the government of Hong Kong. "They all want to go to America." Well, I swear I don't know why, do you? I mean take Vietnam. Why would any Vietnamese come to America after what America did for Vietnam? Don't they remember My Lai, napalm, Sylvester Stallone? Clearly they have no more sense over there than, say, Mexicans who keep trying to get into this country even though this country stole large parts of their country in the first place.

It has been the German army's largest peacetime operation since World War II.

ITN news item

There she is, the huge vast bulk of her.

Wynford Vaughan-Thomas of the BBC, as—unfortunately— the camera moved to a close-up of the late HRH the Queen Mother during the launching of the *Ark Royal*

Dan Rather, during CBS News election night coverage, November 5, 1996

In New Hampshire, closest Senate race in the country, this race between Dick Swett and Bob Smith is hot and tight as a too-small bathing suit on a too-long car ride back from the beach.

Well, am I a liberal, a conservative, or what? What . . . I believe in sunny summer mornings when the grass is sweet and the wind is green with possibilities. I believe in chili with no beans and iced tea all year round . . . I believe music is too important to be left to musicians, and that Ella Fitzgerald is the best American singer ever, and that Beethoven would have liked Chuck Berry . . . And so it goes.

Linda Ellerbee in her first commentary on CNN, March 20, 1989

And so it was woo-woo and goodbye train.

Dan Rather, wrapping up CBS *Evening News*, May 16, 2001, with an item on a runaway freight train

Rolls-Royce announced today that it is recalling all Rolls-Royce cars made after 1966 because of faulty nuts behind the steering wheels.

Walter Cronkite, famously gaffe-prone US anchorman

President Carter has painful hemorrhoids and is being treated by his physician, Rear Admiral, er . . . William Lookass . . . Lukash . . . ?

US newscaster

Thousands may have been gunned down in Beijing, but what about the millions of American kids whose lives are being ruined by an enormous failure of the country's educational system . . . We can and we should agonize about the dead students in Beijing, but we've got a much bigger problem here at home.

John Chancellor's commentary on NBC Nightly *News*, June 20, 1989

The flights, landings and take-off of airships called "flying saucers" and "flying cigars" of any nationality are forbidden on the territory of the community of Châteauneuf-du-Pape.

Decree by the Mayor of Châteauneuf-du-Pape, France October 31, 1954

We are going to play a hiding and finding game. Now, are your balls high up or low down? Close your eyes a minute and dance around, and look for them. Are they high up? Or are they low down? If you have found your balls, toss them over your shoulder and play with them.
Children's radio *Music and Movement* program in the 1950s

So, you're in drapes?
American tourist to John Burton, Surveyor of the Fabric of Westminster Abbey

Too many bugs and leeches and spiders and spider webs. Please spray the wilderness to rid the area of these pests.
Comment on a feedback form from the US Forest Service

She was practicing "fastest finger first" by herself in bed last night.
Chris Tarrant, describing *Who Wants To Be A Millionaire* winner Judith Keppel, on television

I didn't know petrol was highly inflammable.

Taxi driver Saqib Bashir, who bought 21 gallons of gasoline during a fuel shortage in late 2000. Bashir then stored it in plastic containers in an empty house owned by him. The fuel melted the plastic, leaked and fire fighters—alerted by neighbors who could smell fumes—fearing an explosion, evacuated the street in Derby, England. The clean-up operation cost over $150,000.

Pumping is the devil's pastime, and we must all say no to Satan. Inflate your tires by all means, but then hide your bicycle pump where it cannot tempt you.
Spokesman for the Nakhon Ratchasima hospital in Thailand, reported in the *Japan Times*, April 16, 1997

A McDonald's would be nice at the trailhead.
Comment on a feedback form from the US Forest Service

Uri Geller

I was sued by a woman who claimed that she became pregnant because she watched me on television and I bent her contraceptive coil.

What time do the penguins leave the zoo?
Question asked in a tourist information center in Scotland

We have a copy of the list of 1,800 names, and any ex-serviceman wishing to see if his name is on the list can call into the shop under the office and see it.
Notice in the *Western News* and *Galway Leader*, during World War I, giving news that the newspaper had a full list of the men of the Connaught Rangers who had lost their lives

Does the river follow the canyon the whole way down?

Question asked of a river guide accompanying a group rafting down the Colorado River in the Grand Canyon

You guys are working on the Fourth of July? I can't believe it! Don't you celebrate it?

Question asked of an English employee by an American employee of an international company

Listener: My most embarrassing moment was when my artificial leg fell off at the altar on my wedding day.
Simon Fanshawe: How awful! Do you still have an artificial leg?
Exchange on the UK's Talk Radio station

The telephone pole was approaching. I was attempting to swerve out of its way when it struck the front end.

Detail of the "accident in question" in a claim submitted to an insurance company

Did she write anything else?
Question posed to Barnes & Noble staff by a mother whose daughter had just enjoyed *The Diary of Anne Frank*

The guy was all over the road. I had to swerve a number of times before I hit him.

Detail of the "accident in question" in an insurance claim

Interviewer: So did you see which train crashed into which train first?
Fifteen-year-old: No, they both ran into each other at the same time.

Snippet from radio news interview

I am very annoyed that you have branded my son illiterate. This is a dirty lie, as I was married a week before he was born.

Letter to California Department of Human Resource Development

Your food stamps will be stopped effective March 1992 because we received notice that you passed away. May God bless you. You may re-apply if there is a change in your circumstances.

Letter from the Department of Social Services, Greenville, South Carolina

Hereby decreed illegal all: Public flatulence, crepitation, gaseous emission, and miasmic effluence.

Alaskan legislature outlawing the act of "flatulating" (or breaking wind) in public

The most surprising thing about the rehearsal is how Macy (Gray) keeps it together—ringmaster, not freakshow. She is so good at it that she lies down on one of the sofas and simultaneously sings, gives directions and reads a novel. She is both very present and in her own world. Watching her read her book and keep the beat, I realize that it is possible to coexist with humanity and be totally mentally divergent.

Emma Forest, reporting in the *Telegraph Magazine*— sent into "Pseuds' Corner" section of *Private Eye*

Can you copy the Internet onto this disk for me?
Customer in a computer shop

Coming home I drove into the wrong house and collided with a tree I don't have.
Detail of the "accident in question" in a claim submitted to an insurance company

He called attention to the number of ownerless dogs about the streets, and urged that the police should have instructions to destroy them, or order dogs, with owners, to be muzzled.
From the *Birmingham Daily Post*, in the nineteenth century

The captain swum ashore from the vessel and subsequently saved the life of the stewardess; she was insured for fifteen thousand dollars and was full of railroad iron.
Notice in a nineteenth-century newspaper

MISQUOTES AND MISPRINST

No entry for heavy goods vehicles.
Residential site only.
I am not in the office at the moment.
Send any work to be translated.
Dual language road sign near Swansea in Wales written in English and Welsh. Unfortunately the non-Welsh speaking sign-writing team got an out-of-office response from their Welsh translator reading: *Nid wyd yn y swyddfa ar hyn o bryd. Anfonwch unrhyw waith i'w gyfieithu*—and they thought he'd sent them the translation. The sign was erected by non-Welsh speakers in South Wales, much to the amusement of the Welsh speakers.

This afternoon there will be a meeting in the south and north ends of the church. Children will be baptized at both ends.
Church bulletin

The Red Cross paid for emergency care and later found a free bed for her in an institution specializing in the treatment of artcritics.
Arizona Star

Today Lesbian forces invaded . . . no, sorry, that should be Lesbianese.
From a British news report on the conflict in Lebanon

A squid, as you know, of course, has ten testicles.

Graham Kerr, Canadian TV chef on the cookery program *The Galloping Gourmet*

The ladies of the church have cast off clothing of every kind. They can be seen in the church basement this Saturday.
Church bulletin

Beware! To touch these wires is instant death. Anyone found doing so will be prosecuted.
Sign at a US railroad station

Ladies and gentlemen: the President of the United States—Hoobert Herver!
American radio announcer Harry von Zell, welcoming President Herbert Hoover at the microphone

You be libertas, I be patria.

How the *Washington Post* reported the famous Latin phrase *Ubi libertas, ibi patria*, pronounced by a certain Mr. Curtis as he unveiled the Sedgewick Monument at West Point

He was of *accidental* character, and the jury returned a verdict of *excellent* death.
English country newspaper in the nineteenth century

Remember in prayer the many who are sick of our church and community.

Slip-up in the delivery of the usual notices during a church service

You are now going to hear the bum of the flightelbee.

Stuart Hibberd, radio announcer

The choir invites any member of the congregation who enjoys sinning to join the choir.

Church bulletin, with an unfortunate misprint

I didn't intend for this to take on a political tone. I'm just here for the drugs.

Nancy Reagan, replying to an unwelcome and unrelated question at a "Just Say No" campaign event

Ousted chief of the Royal Society for the Prevention of Cruelty to Animals says he was a scapegoat.

An item in *The Times*

The Fire Brigade was soon on the scene, and once they commenced to turn their noses onto the flames the conflagration was soon under control.
Egyptian Mail

Police superintendent Geoffrey Squire, aged 42, of Brynfrydd Close, Coychurch, fined $55 by Bridgend magistrates after admitting carless driving in Aberkenfig on October 28.
South Wales Echo

Concert promoters MCP have donated three pairs of tickets for the Princes Hall show. All you have to do is answer the following question: With which band did Midge have his No. 2 hit *Vienna* in 1981?

Answers to:
Ultravox Competition,
the 'News', 4, High Street,
Camberley, Surrey

The pot growers had tapped into an irrigation line for landscaping around the gated community of Stoneridge, and had rigged up a network of white PVC piping to grow the cannibals.
Orange County Register

"This budget leakage is something that's got to stop," said the President, with what seemed to be more than a trace of irrigation in his voice.
Jackson State Times

In our report of the Welsh National Opera's *Cavalleria Rusticana* and *Pagliacci*, the computer spellchecker did not recognize the term WNO (Welsh National Opera). A slip of the finger caused it to be replaced with the word 'winos'.
The Guardian

A front-page article yesterday about the role that Barack Obama's wife, Michelle, is playing in his presidential campaign rendered incorrectly a word in a quotation from Valerie Jarrett, a friend of the Obamas who commented on their decision that he would run. She said in a telephone interview, "Barack and Michelle thought long and hard about this decision before they made it"—not that they "fought" long and hard.
New York Times

A picture caption on Wednesday with an article about a meeting between the leaders of North Korea and South Korea misspelled the name of the North Korean capital, where the meeting was held. It is Pyongyang, not Pongyang.
New York Times

Mothers Help wanted to help with children and lighthouse work
East Grinstead News in Focus

Mai Thai Finn is one of the students in the program and was in the center of the photo. We incorrectly listed her name as one of the items on the menu.
Community Life

By an unfortunate typographical error in Prisea Middlemiss's article last Wednesday, Professor Ian Macgillivray and two of his colleagues were described as "abortion obstetricians" instead of "Aberdeen obstetricians". We apologize to the doctors concerned.

The Guardian

In our story on London Hosts, the Grand Met managed house operation, it was stated that the "Pub 80" concept probably appealed more to the younger drinker or those looking for bad food. This should, of course, have read "Bar food." We apologize for any embarrassment caused.
Morning Advertiser

We incorrectly called Mary Ann Thompson Frenk a socialist. She is a socialite.

Dallas Morning News

The authorities at Ongar library have received a number of complaints about a card in the index file with an entry which read: SEX: SEE LIBRARIAN. This has now been changed. The new entry reads: SEX: FOR SEX ASK AT THE DESK.
Eastern Gazette

Alan Greenspan in hospital for an enlarged prostitute.
ABC TV News caption

The British and American proposals for a transfer to majority rule provides for a constitution based on universal suffering.

New Nigerian

When Redding, a longtime scout for *Playboy*, discovered Smith, the model could barely **right** a sentence.

Houston Chronicle

The Guardian

Relieved officials from Sarkozy's ruling UMP party yesterday hoped the quick wedding and Bruni's new official status would stem his plummeting approval ratings. At 41 percent, they are his lowest ratings since his election—and owe much to his slowness to push through convincing economic reforms and his very pubic romance.

Heavy overnight fishing in El Salvador's strategic southeastern Unsulutan Province was reported by military sources Monday as left-wing guerrillas switched the focus of their attacks from the north.
Athens News

We apologize for the error in last week's paper in which we stated that Mr. Arnold Dogbody was a defective in the police force. We meant, of course, that Mr. Dogbody is a detective in the police farce.

Correction notice in the *Ely Standard*, Cambridgeshire, England

Naval elements of Iran's Revolutionary Guard equipped with high speed lunches are based on the nearby island of Larak, now Iran's main oil terminal.

The Observer

In many parts of Co. Sligo hares are now practically unknown because of the unreasonable laughter to which they have been subjected in recent years.

Sligo Times

Erratum: The word "ambiguity" in our second leading article yesterday, should have been "anti-guity."

The Natal Mercury, June 22, 1883, correcting an article from the previous day in which mention had been made of the world's "wonted tokens of ambiguity." The day afterwards, the following appeared in the paper: "Double Erratum: The unknown word 'anti-guity' in a local paragraph yesterday professing to correct the word 'ambiguity', should have been 'antiquity'"

DOING THE BUSINESS

The nature of any human being, certainly anyone on Wall Street, is "the **better** deal you give the customer, the **worse** deal it is for you."

Bernard Madoff

This company is not bust. We are merely in a cyclical decline.

Lord Stokes, then Chairman of ailing firm British Leyland. *The Observer* newspaper, "Quotes of the Year," 1974

Had cancer, been a pain, now pregnant.

Management meeting at Schroder Salomon Smith Barney summing up the career of employee Julie Bower in June 2002— who then sued them and won $2.1m

We don't pay taxes. Only the little people pay taxes.

Leona Helmsley (dubbed "the Queen of Mean"), widow and heir of the New York real estate tycoon, Henry Helmsley, and one of the richest women in the United States. Helmsley was convicted of mail fraud and tax evasion in the 1990s and was sentenced to 18 months' imprisonment

Murdoch is a monster.
Charles Douglas-Home, describing Rupert Murdoch before accepting the editorship of *The Times* newspaper under . . . the very same media tycoon

Edsger Dijkstra
The question of whether computers can think is like the question of whether submarines can swim.

As far as we know, our computer has never had an undetected error.

Weisert

I think that's a bit too many. I don't think there are 49 Finns that can sing.
Alain Levy, Chief Executive of EMI Records, after the ailing company, which had shed 1,800 jobs, discovered how many artists it had under contract in Finland

I'll tell you, it's Big Business. If there is one word to describe Atlantic City, it's Big Business. Or two words—Big Business.
Donald Trump, real estate tycoon

In today's regulatory environment, it's virtually impossible to violate rules...but it's impossible for a violation to go undetected, certainly not for a considerable period of time.
Disgraced financier Bernard Madoff, speaking on a panel called "The Future of the Stock Market" in New York on October 20, 2007

Efforts to assign a primary causal role to tobacco use on the basis of statistical associations ignore all the unknowns and focus undue attention on tobacco use.
Clarence Cook Little, Director of the Tobacco Industry Research Committee, in 1958

I don't know that I'm in the twentieth century—I may be in the eighteenth or twenty-first.
Ian Macgregor, Chairman of British Steel, January 1981

We've got to pause and ask ourselves: How much clean air do we need?
Lee Iacocca, chairman of the Chrysler Corporation

Question: Do you support the overthrow of the government by force, subversion, or violence?
Respondent: Violence.
Allegedly genuine entry, on a prospective employee's job application form

I'm a bit of a Barnum. I make stars out of everyone.
Donald Trump, on his former lovers

It needs to be said that the poor are poor
because they don't have enough money.

**Sir Keith Joseph, one of Margaret Thatcher's trusted
advisors, speaking in March 1970**

Donald Trump

The point is
that you can't be
too greedy.

History is more or less bunk. It's tradition.

Henry Ford, in an interview with Charles N. Wheeler in 1916

They don't suffer. They
can't even speak English.
George F. Baer, railroad industrialist,
answering a reporter's question about
the plight of starving miners

We're going to try to get the boys out of the trenches
by Christmas. I've chartered a ship, and some of us
are going to Europe.

Henry Ford in 1915—a comment which resulted in
the newspaper headline, "Great War Ends Christmas
Day. Ford To Stop It"

No Va.

The reason the Chevrolet Nova, manufactured by General Motors, was selling so slowly in Spanish-speaking countries was because the ad was telling consumers, it "Won't Go" (No Va). Vauxhall subsequently fell into the same trap with its hatchback of the same name

E-mail is not to be used to pass on information or data. It should only be used for company business. Memo from the accounting manager, Electric Boat Company

We will never make a 32-bit operating system.
Bill Gates, Microsoft CEO, at the launch of MSX

No one really understands what's going on with all these numbers.

David Stockman, business whiz kid and Reagan advisor, in a foolishly frank interview given to a reporter from the *Atlantic Monthly* in 1981. It was one of many unguarded gaffes (most famously, "Reaganomics aren't working") made by him

As of tomorrow, employees will only be able to access the building using individual security cards. Pictures will be taken next Wednesday and employees will receive their cards in two weeks.
Sun Microsystems memo

What I need is a list of specific, unknown problems we will encounter.
Memo from Lykes Lines Shipping

R&D supervisor, 3M Corporation

Doing it right is no excuse for not meeting the schedule. No one will believe you solved this problem in **one day!** We've been working on it for months. Now, go act busy for a few weeks and I'll let you know when it's time to tell them.

How Anyone Can Stop Paying Income Taxes
Title of 1983 American bestseller by Irwin Schiff (the IRS shortly afterwards issued him with a bill for $200,000)

I think there is a world market for maybe five computers.
Thomas Watson, chairman of IBM in 1943

Pepsi brings your ancestors back from the grave.

Foolish translation for the Chinese version of a US poster campaign for Pepsi, which in America had read, "Come Alive with Pepsi." (In Germany, the slogan was only marginally better: "Come alive out of the grave with Pepsi")

You had a lot of novice investors who got into the market looking for easy money, without any regard to the fundamentals. These stocks were running on fumes.
Bernard Madoff talking about the Dot.com boom and bust (*Washington Post*, January 2, 2001). Madoff is alleged to have taken $2 billion of Banco Sanatander's money…

A man who has a million dollars is as well off as if he were rich.
John Jacob Astor, US property tycoon and one of the most famous casualties of the *Titanic*

Stocks have reached what looks like a permanently high plateau.
Irving Fisher, Professor of Economics, Yale University, speaking on October 17, 1929—the Wall Street Crash occurred on October 29, 1929

Get your feet off my desk, get out of here, you stink, and we're not going to buy your product.
Joe Keenan, president of Atari, to Steve Jobs, 1976

So we went to Atari and said, "Hey, we've got this amazing thing, even built with some of your parts, and what do you think about funding us? Or we'll give it to you. We just want to do it. Pay our salary, we'll come work for you." And they said, "No." So then we went to Hewlett-Packard, and they said, "Hey, we don't need you. You haven't got through college yet."
Steve Jobs, Apple Computer Inc. co-founder, on attempts to muster interest in his and Steve Wozniak's personal computer

A receptacle having at least one exterior surface and a plurality of walls defining a discrete object receiving volume.

An (unnamed) lawyer's suggested phrasing, in a patent application, with which to replace the word "container."

Richard Kelly, US Congressman

I can see (the dumping of waste) to be a benefit, otherwise you will end up with lots of vast, empty gravel pits all over the country.
Ed Oakley, Chief Purchasing Officer for McDonald's UK, on the company's supposedly green recycling policy, during the "McLibe!" trial

I think that the free enterprise system is absolutely too important to be left to the voluntary action of the market place.

A short lease means a lease which is not a long lease.
Blindingly obvious phrase in Income Tax Act, 1952

This was a very large corporation. It would be impossible to know everything going on.
Jeffrey K. Skilling, formerly chief executive of the now-disgraced Enron

This project is important; we can't let things that are more important interfere with it.
Useful suggestion on how to learn to prioritize by advertising manager, United Parcel Service

Beginners will find that the computer is logical to a disagreeable and intensely frustrating degree.
Student notes for OSIRIS II

Teamwork is a lot of people doing what "I" say.
Marketing executive, Citrix Corporation, demonstrating how to be a team player

If there are any points on which you require explanation or further particulars we shall be glad to furnish such additional details as may be required by telephone. In other words, "ring us if you have any further queries"

The benefit of having dedicated subject matter experts who are able to evangelize the attributes and business imperatives of their products is starting to bear fruit.
Announcement related to company restructuring by Marconi's EMEA (Europe, Middle East, Africa and Australasia) division

Lucent is endeavorily [sic] determined to promote constant attention on current procedures of transacting business focusing emphasis on innovative ways to better, if not supersede, the expectations of quality.
Statement from Lucent Technologies

Bill Gates

There are people who don't like capitalism, and people who don't like PCs. But there's no one who likes the PC who doesn't like Microsoft.

A cookie store is a bad idea. Besides, the market research reports say America likes crispy cookies, not soft and chewy cookies like you make.
Response to Debbi Fields' idea of launching Mrs. Fields' Cookies as a business venture

It is a project which, as far as I can see, has a viable marketing opportunity ahead of it.
Giles Shaw, Northern Ireland Minister of Commerce, speaking in 1979 about the De Lorean—the motor car nobody wanted to buy (except the makers of the *Back to the Future* films)

BRANIFF MEANS BUSINESS.
Advertisement in *The Times* newspaper on May 13 , 1982—unfortunately, the day after the airline had gone bust

Everett Dirksen

A billion here, a billion there—sooner or later it adds up to real money.

They're multi-purpose. Not only do they put the clips **on**, but they take them **off**.

Explanation from Pratt & Whitney on why they charged the US Air Force nearly $1,000 for a pair of pliers

Lunch and Learn Seminar: "Who's controlling your life?" (Get your manager's permission before attending.)

Flyer promoting attendance at a corporate seminar

We know that communication is a problem. But the company is not going to discuss it with the employees.

Switching supervisor, AT&T Long Lines Division

John Hinnes, chief executive of An Post

That mail that used to be handled by hand, now it's handled manually.

640K ought to be enough for anybody.
Attributed to Bill Gates, Microsoft CEO, in 1981, but
believed to be an urban myth

**Nothing sucks like
an Electrolux!**
Electrolux's first marketing campaign for the firm's
vacuum cleaners in the US. The Swedish-speaking
team who came up with the slogan didn't realize
that "sucks" is not the greatest virtue
in the United States

This is the end of Western civilization.
Lewis Douglas, US budget director, on
learning that Franklin D. Roosevelt was
intending to take the United States off the
gold standard in 1933

**Could we have a crash à
la 1929? The flat
answer is "no."**
Dr. Pierre A. Rinfret, economics
expert, quoted in *Time* magazine,
October 5, 1987—"Black Monday"
followed shortly after, on October 19.
Superceded by the Global Financial
Meltdown in 2008–09

20/20 HINDSIGHT

Elizabeth Taylor, speaking in 1982

I'll never get married again.

God himself could not sink this ship.
Deckhand on the *Titanic*, which sank on the night of April 14, 1912, on her maiden voyage

With over fifty foreign cars already on sale here, the Japanese auto industry isn't likely to carve out a big slice of the US market.
Prediction by *Business Week*, August 1968

Guitar groups are on the way out.
Dick Rowe of Decca Records rejecting the Beatles

Television won't be able to hold on to any market it captures after the first six months. People will soon get tired of staring at a plywood box every night.
Darryl Zanuck, executive at 20th Century Fox, 1946

...Nor are computers going to get much faster.

Dr Arthur L. Samuel,
"The Banishment of
Paper Work,"
New Scientist, 1964

With all of the hysteria, all of the fear, all of the phony science, could it be that man-made global warming is the greatest hoax ever perpetrated on the American people? It sure sounds like it. James M. Inhofe, speech in US Senate, July 28, 2003

Nuclear-powered vacuum cleaners will probably be a reality within ten years.
Alex Lewyt, president of Lewyt vacuum company, 1955

The problem with television is that the people must sit and keep their eyes glued to a screen; the average American family hasn't time for it.

The New York Times, 1939

I don't think there'll be war. The Führer doesn't want his new buildings bombed.
Unity Mitford, Adolf Hitler's English "companion," in 1938

Apple is already dead.

Nathan Myhrvold, former Microsoft CTO speaking in
tribute of what he though was their "former" rival in 1997

To assert that the earth revolves around the sun is as erroneous [as] to claim that Jesus was not born of a virgin.

Cardinal Belleramine

No mere machine can replace a reliable and honest clerk.

Remington Arms Co., dismissing a newfangled invention that had been given the name "typewriter"

Lord Tanlaw, May 1977

By the end of 1991, it is not unreasonable to suppose, driving will become an occupation indulged in by the super-rich, just as it was in the early 1920s.

We just won't have arthritis in 2000.
Dr. William Clark, president of the Arthritis Foundation, 1966

The Americans have need of the telephone, but we [British] do not. We have plenty of messenger boys.
Sir William Preece

Speaking movies are impossible. When a century has passed, all thought of our so-called "talking pictures" will have been abandoned. It will never be possible to synchronize the voice with the picture.
D.W. Griffiths, movie mogul, 1926

It is quite clear to me that the Tory Party will get rid of Mrs. Thatcher in about three years' time.
Harold Wilson, former Labour Prime Minister, speaking in 1980, a year after she was elected. Thatcher would go on to win three general elections

I have not the smallest molecule of faith in aerial navigation other than ballooning.
Lord Kelvin, Victorian physicist and President of the Royal Society, 1896

Television won't matter in your lifetime or mine.
Rex Lambert, Editor of *The Listener* journal, writing in 1936

This "telephone" has too many shortcomings to be seriously considered as a means of communication. The device is inherently of no value to us.
Western Union Telegraph Company, internal memo, 1876

I have traveled the length and breadth of this country and talked with the best people . . . and I can assure you that data processing is a fad that won't last out the year.
Editor in charge of business books for Prentice Hall publishers, 1957

There is not the slightest indication that nuclear energy will ever be obtainable. It would mean that the atom would have to be shattered at will.
Albert Einstein, in 1932, proving that he wasn't a genius 24/7

The atomic bomb will **never** go off, and I speak as an expert in explosives.
Admiral William Leahy, on the US Atomic Bomb Project, to President Truman in 1945

That is the biggest fool thing we have ever done . . . The bomb will never go off.
President Harry S. Truman, shortly after assuming office, when he was briefed on the Manhattan Project to develop atomic weapons. (He subsequently ordered the atomic bombs dropped on Hiroshima and Nagasaki to end World War II with Japan)

No audience will ever be able to take more than ten minutes of animation.
Walt Disney executive, considering the viability of an animated movie called *Snow White and the Seven Dwarfs*

Four or five frigates will do the business without any military force.
Lord North, addressing the House of Commons at the outbreak of the American Revolution (1774)

Simon Newcomb, US astronomer, 1902

Flight by machines heavier than air is unpractical, and insignificant, if not utterly impossible.

Rail travel at high speed is not possible because passengers, unable to breathe, would die of asphyxia.
Dr. Dionysus Lardner, Professor of Natural Philosophy and Astronomy at University College, London

Everything that can be invented has been invented.
Charles H. Duell, Commissioner of the US Office of Patents, 1899

You will be home before the leaves have fallen from the trees.

Kaiser Wilhelm, encouraging departing German troops at the outbreak of World War I

Lawn tennis, though an excellent game in every respect is, nevertheless, one in which middle-aged people, especially ladies, cannot engage with satisfaction to themselves, and its rapidly waning popularity is largely due to this fact.
The Isthmian Book of Croquet, 1899

The wireless music box has no imaginable commercial value. Who would pay for a message sent to nobody in particular?

David Sarnoff's associates in response to his urgings for investment in the radio in the 1920s

The concept is interesting and well formed, but in order to earn better than a "C," the idea must be feasible.
A Yale University management professor in response to Fred Smith's paper proposing reliable overnight delivery service. Smith went on to found Federal Express.

It would be found altogether useless in practice, because the power being applied in the stern, it would be absolutely impossible to make the vessel steer.
Sir William Symonds, Surveyor of HM Navy, on propeller-driven ships, in 1837

Before man reaches the moon your mail will be delivered within hours from New York to Australia by **guided missiles**. We stand on the threshold of rocket mail.
Arthur Summerfield, US Postmaster General under President Eisenhower, in 1959

Louis Pasteur's theory of germs is a ridiculous fiction.
Pierre Pochet, Professor of Physiology at Toulouse, 1872

There is no hope for the fanciful idea of reaching the moon, because of insurmountable barriers to escaping the earth's gravity.
Dr. F.R. Moulton, University of Chicago astronomer, 1932

There will never be a bigger plane built.
A Boeing engineer, after the first flight of the 247, a twin-engined airplane that held ten people

Airplanes are interesting toys but of no military value.
Ferdinand Foch, Professor of Strategy, École Supérieure de Guerre, 1911

Earlier, a woman apparently called the BBC and said there's going to be a hurricane... well, don't worry, there isn't. But there will be some strong winds in Spain and across to France.

BBC weatherman Michael Fish, predicting a quiet night for the South of England on October 15 , 1987. The "Great Storm" that battered Southern England that night was the worst in 300 years, killing 18 people and flattening 15 million trees.

I do not think we shall hear much more of the general strike in our life.

Ramsay Macdonald, *The Observer* "Sayings of the Week," May 1926

Pish! A woman might piss it out.

Lord Mayor of London, on being told in the small hours of the morning of September 13, 1666, of a blaze in Pudding Lane. The Great Fire of London ensued

But what . . . is it good for?

Robert Lloyd, engineer at the Advanced Computing Systems Division of IBM, 1968, commenting on the microchip

In all likelihood, world inflation is over.

Dr. Per Jacobsson, Managing Director of the IMF (International Monetary Fund), in October 1959

There is no reason anyone would want a computer in their home.

Ken Olson, president, chairman and founder of Digital Equipment Corporation, at the 1977 Convention of the World Future Society in Boston

In my opinion, she's nix.

Howard Hughes, director, on actress Jean Harlow, who was then still called Harlean Carpenter (his opinion was shared by screenwriter Joseph March, who declared, "My God, she's got a shape like a dustpan")

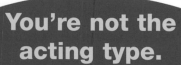

You're not the acting type.

Headmaster of Pembroke Lodge School to a certain schoolboy by the name of Alec Guinness

He hasn't got any future.

Rejection letter to John Le Carré, author of *The Spy Who Came in from the Cold* and *Smiley's People*

> They are doomed to an early and expensive death.
>
> **A.P. Herbert, writer for London-based *Punch* magazine, forecasting an end to talking films**

I predict the Internet will soon go spectacularly supernova and in 1996 catastrophically collapse.
Robert Metcalfe, *InfoWorld* magazine, 1995

Man will not be able to fly for at least another fifty years.
Wright brothers, pioneers of powered, manned flight, 1901

Aujourd'hui, rien (today, nothing).
Diary entry from Louis XVI, King of France, on July 14, 1789—the day the Bastille was stormed

Two years from now, spam will be solved.

Bill Gates, founder of Microsoft, 2004

Do not bother to sell your gas shares. The electric light has **no future.**
Professor John Henry Pepper on Thomas Edison's electric light invention

Thomas Edison, in 1926
I have determined that there is no market for talking pictures.

It is impossible to transmit speech electrically. The "telephone" is as **mythical** as the unicorn.
Professor Johann Christian Poggendorff, German physicist and chemist, 1860

When the Paris Exhibition closes, electric light will close with it and no more will be heard of it.
Professor Erasmus Wilson of Oxford University, 1878

What can be more palpably absurd and ridiculous than the prospect held out of locomotives travelling twice as fast as stage coaches!
Comment in *Quarterly Review*, March 1825

TURNING THE TEAM AROUND 360 DEGREES

Colin had a **hard on** in practice earlier, and I bet he wishes he had a **hard on** now.
Jack Burnicle on superbike racer Colin Edwards's choice of hard or soft tire

Alan Ball

I'm not a believer in luck. . . but I do believe you need it.

We must have had 99 percent of the possession. It was the other three per cent that cost us.
Ruud Gullitt

John Motson

Nearly all the Brazilian supporters are wearing yellow shirts. It's a fabulous kaleidoscope of color.

Sao Paulo is predictably variable.
Car racing pundit Mark Blundell on the vagaries of the Interlagos circuit

This is like déjà vu all over again.

"Yogi" Berra, baseball legend (former New York Yankee and Mets player and coach)—the man widely attributed to have introduced the phrase, "It ain't over till it's over"

Ralph, I would like to be able to tell the folks what happened on that play, but the Florida cheerleaders were **shaking their fuzzy things** right in front of us.

University of Kentucky commentator Cawood Ledford on the intervention of pompoms

When I said they'd scored **two** goals, of course I meant they'd scored **one**.

George Hamilton, Irish football commentator

Derek Johnstone on BBC Scotland

He's one of those soccer players whose brains are in his head.

You're next, big mouth.

Sonny Liston to Cassius Clay, soon to be known as Muhammed Ali, after defeating Floyd Patterson in 1963. Ali subsequently gave Sonny Liston a whupping

He's got such a balanced pair of shoulders with an old head.
Mark Blundell describing the youngest ever Grand Prix winner, Sebastian Vettel

If Glenn Hoddle said **one word** to his team at half-time, it was concentration and focus.

Ron Atkinson

This is the biggest thing that's happened in Athens since Homer put down his pen.
John Motson

Michael Owen— he's got the legs of a salmon.
Sky TV commentator, on UK soccer player

The word "genius" isn't applicable in football. A genius is a guy like Norman Einstein.
Joe Theisman, former quarterback for the Washington Redskins and sports commentator (Theisman did explain later that a former classmate had this name)

We're going to turn this team around 360 degrees.
Jason Kidd, after his drafting to US basketball team the Dallas Mavericks

We estimate, and this isn't an estimation, that Greta Waitz is 80 seconds behind.
David Coleman, sports commentator, famous for his gaffes—dubbed "Colemanballs" by satirical magazine *Private Eye*

That Michael Jackson is amazing! Three plays in two minutes!
Al Gore, commenting at a basketball game in which Michael Jordan was playing

The Americans sowed the seed, and now they have reaped the whirlwind.
Sebastian (now Lord) Coe, former Olympic medallist for middle-distance running

Murray Walker, car-racing commentator

And now the boot is on the other Schumacher!

I would like to thank my parents—especially my father and mother.
Part of golfer Greg Norman's winning speech at the 1983 World Matchplay Championship

Raikkonen would have been on pole if he hadn't have made two critical mistakes, so if he can take that consistency (into the race), he stands a chance.
Mark Blundell before the 2008 French Grand Prix

My favorite part was when the other team scored a football and then we came right back on the next play and scored a football, too.
Kathleen Kennedy Townsend, Maryland Lt. Governor and member of the Kennedy clan, during the Super Bowl in 2001 (what she should have said was, "a touchdown")

Done, through, washed-up.
Verdict in the *Atlanta Constitution* on Jack Nicklaus; a week later, the "Golden Bear" won the 1986 US Masters championship

With eight minutes left, the game could be won in the next five or ten minutes.

Jimmy Armfield, radio commentator

John Hollins

A contract on a piece of paper, saying you want to leave, is like a piece of paper saying you want to leave.

The marshals are trying to extradite Sato from his car.
Car racing pundit
Mark Blundell

Oh, that's good running on the run.
John Motson

Andy Hinchcliffe

Our consistency's been all over the place.

I can't really remember the names of the clubs that we went to.
Shaquille O'Neal, replying to an interviewer who had asked whether he had visited the Parthenon during his recent trip to Greece

I've lost count of how many chances
Helsingborg have had. It's at least five.
John Motson

You guys line up
alphabetically by height.
Bill Peterson, Florida
State football coach

You can just see a little **crack** start
to appear in the **paperwork**.
Mark Blundell talking about the pressure on
former F1 World Champion Fernando Alonso

One of the reasons
Arnie [Arnold Palmer] is
playing so well is that, before each
tee-shot, his wife takes out his balls
and **kisses** them—Oh my God,
what have I just said?
US golf commentator

This is really a lovely horse.
I once rode her mother.
Ted Walsh, racing commentator

It's never happened in the World Series
competition, and it still hasn't.
Yogi Berra, baseball legend

We now have exactly
the same situation as we had at
the start of the race, only exactly
the opposite.
**Murray Walker, car-racing
commentator**

The only problem I really have
in the outfield is with flyballs.
**Carmelo Martinez, San Diego
Padres outfield player**

Casey Stengel,
baseball legend

They brought me
up to the Brooklyn
Dodgers, which at
that time was
in Brooklyn.

It's now 1-1, an exact reversal
of the score on Saturday.
Radio 5 Live commentator

I'd find the fellow who lost it, and, if he was poor, I'd return it.

Yogi Berra, when asked what he would do if he found a million dollars

It's a drag having to wear socks during matches, because the tan, like, stops at the ankles. I can never get my skin, like, color coordinated.

Monica Seles

She won't win a game.

Fred Perry on Billie-Jean King before the tennis match against Bobby Riggs in 1973. (She did)

Andy Gray, soccer commentator, on Arsenal's manager

If you gave Arsène Wenger eleven players and told him to pick his team, this would be it.

He is accelerating all the time. That last lap was run in 64 seconds and the one before in 62.

David Coleman, sports commentator

I want to keep fighting because it is the only thing that keeps me out of hamburger joints. If I don't fight, I'll eat this planet.
George Foreman

Lawrie Sanchez

It's nice for us to have a fresh face in the camp to bounce things off.

There's no doubt in my mind that if the race had been 46 laps instead of 45 it would have been a McLaren first and second. But it didn't, so it wasn't.
Murray Walker, car-racing commentator

Alan Brazil

I have seen players sent off for far worse offenses than that.

If you don't know where you are going, you will wind up somewhere else.
Yogi Berra, baseball legend

And some 500 Italians made the trip, in a crowd of only 400.
Radio Commentator

I think I can win. I've got nothing better to do this weekend.
David Feherty before the 1994 Open Golf Championship.
(He lost)

The par here at Sunningdale is 70 and anything under that will mean a score in the sixties.
Steve Rider, golf presenter

If you'd offered me a 69 at the start this morning I'd have been all over you.
Sam Torrance, former Ryder Cup captain

Yogi Berra

It was impossible to get a conversation going; everybody was talking too much.

Well, that was a cliff-dweller.
Wes Westrum, Mets coach, commentating
on a tense baseball moment

Mick Lyons

**If there wasn't such a thing as football,
we'd all be frustrated footballers.**

And the line-up for the final of the
Women's 400 meters hurdles includes
three Russians, two East Germans, a
Pole, a Swede and a **Frenchman**.
David Coleman, BBC sports commentator

**And it's Mansell . . .
Mansell . . . Nigel Mansell!**
Murray Walker, apoplectic with excitement
while describing the 1990 Monaco Grand
Prix—only to realize in a fit of apologies
that viewers were actually watching
Frenchman Alain Prost

Steve Coppell

I am not going to make
it a **target**, but it's
something to **aim** for.

I would like to thank the press from the **heart** of my **bottom.**

Nick Faldo's winning speech after his 1992 Open championship win

Hodge scored for Forest after 22 seconds ~ totally against the run of play.

Peter Lorenzo

I don't think he's ever lost a race at 200 meters, except at 400.
David Coleman, covering the 1992 Olympic Games

The young Ralf Schumacher has been upstaged by the teenager, Jenson Button, who is twenty.
Murray Walker, car-racing commentator

I can see the **carrot** at the end of the tunnel.
Stuart Pearce

> **Merseyside derbies usually last 90 minutes and I'm sure today's won't be any different.**
> Trevor Booking, TV soccer commentator

> Bob Taylor, UK soccer player

As a striker, you are either in a purple patch or struggling. At the moment, I'm somewhere in between.

And Arsenal now have plenty of time to dictate the last few seconds.
Peter Jones, soccer commentator

Her time is about 4.33, which she's capable of.
David Coleman, sports commentator

. . . and so they have not been able to improve their 100 percent record.
Sports Roundup

The girls in front are breaking wind.
Anonymous US commentator on the women's cycling
event at the 1984 Los Angeles Olympics

Norman
Whiteside

The only thing I
have in common
with George Best is
that we come from
the same place . . .
play for the same
club . . . and were
discovered by the
same man.

It just as easily
could have gone
the other way.
Don Zimmer, Chicago
Cubs manager, on his
team's 4–4 record

**Maths is totally done
differently to what I was
taught when I was at school.
David Beckham
(and English was probably taught
differently as well)**

If you can't make the putts and can't get the
man in from second on the bottom of the
ninth, you're not going to win enough football
games in this league, and that's the problem
we had today.
Sam Rutigliano, coach for the Cleveland
Browns, explaining in clear,
concise terms why his team had lost

David Acfield

Strangely, in slow motion replay, the ball seemed to hang in the air for even longer.

I did not think Patrick deserved to be sent off. He didn't really touch the player because he's not in hospital.
Arsène Wenger defending the on-pitch actions of Patrick Vieira.

Do my eyes deceive me or is Senna's car sounding a bit rough?
Murray Walker, car-racing commentator

I'd say he's done more than that.
Yogi Berra, when asked if first baseman Don Mattingly had exceeded expectations for the current season

The Republic of China—back in the Olympic Games for the first time.
David Coleman, BBC sports commentator

There goes Juantorena down the back straight, opening his legs and showing his class.

David Coleman, commentating during The Montreal Olympics

Yeah, but we're making great time!

Yogi Berra, in reply to, "Hey Yogi, I think we're lost"

That's the fastest time ever run—but it's not as fast as the world record.

David Coleman, BBC sports commentator

Clinton Morrison

I'd been ill and hadn't trained for a week and I'd been out of the team for three weeks before that, so I wasn't sharp. I got cramp before half-time as well. But I'm not one to make excuses.

A mediocre season for Nelson Piquet, as he is now known, and always has been.

Murray Walker, car-racing commentator.
(Piquet is not his real name—it's Nelson Soutomaior)

He's signalling to the bench with his **groin.**

Mark Bright

No regrets, none at all. My only regret is that we went out on penalties. That's my only regret but no, no regrets.

Mick McCarthy

I've never had major knee surgery on any other part of my body.

Winston Bennett, former University of Kentucky basketball forward

That's football, Mike, Northern Ireland have had several chances and haven't scored, but England have had no chances and scored twice.

Trevor Brooking

Glenn Hoddle

Every team has a blimp during the season and it's how you react to that blimp that's important.

Glenn Hoddle

Steven Carr has hit a small blimp but we're hoping that he'll be back on course in the near future.

Tambay's hopes, which were previously nil, are now absolutely zero. Murray Walker, car-racing commentator

Ron Greenwood

In comparison, there's no comparison.

They (Leeds) used to be like Arsenal, winning by one goal to nil—or even less. Nasser Hussain on Channel 5

And there's no damage to the car. Except to the car itself.
Murray Walker, whose autobiography *Unless I'm Very Much Mistaken* said it all

Moses Kiptanui, the 19-year-old Kenyan, who turned 20 a few weeks ago.

David Coleman, sports commentator

We've got tailbacks on the M6. That's been caused by the sheer weight of **Trafford** heading for **Old Traffic**.
Talksport Traffic Newsreader

Paul Gascoigne

I never make predictions and I never will.

This is an interesting circuit because it has inclines. And not just up, but down as well.
Murray Walker, car-racing commentator

Martin Hodge

I spent four indifferent years at Goodison Park, but they were great years.

Yes, it's true, I said "black shit" but he (Vieira) provoked me by saying "gypsy s**t." I called him black but I might just as well have called him French . . . I didn't want to insult him because of the color of his skin just as I'm sure he didn't want to insult me by calling me a gypsy . . . I did call him "black bastard," but I didn't call him a monkey. He doesn't look like a monkey, but if he did I would probably have called him that.

Sinisa Mihajlovic, doing his bit to promote racial harmony within European soccer.

We say "educated left foot" . . . of course, there are many players with educated right foots.

Ron Jones, on *Radio 5 Live*

I imagine the conditions in those cars are totally unimaginable.

Murray Walker, car-racing commentator

The lead car is absolutely unique—except for the car behind, which is **identical.**

Murray Walker, car-racing commentator

They were fourth division grounds but they haven't changed since they changed the name of the league, so they are, by definition, fourth division grounds.

Gabby Yorath, TV host

One coach was training a player's hair, and another was training another part of his body.
Claudio Ranieri, commenting on Chelsea's soccer training method

John Francombe, jockey

The race course is as level as a billiard ball.

Monet was born in Le Havre or Paris, or was brought up there and then went to Paris to do his painting.
Tour de France commentator David Duffield

There's nothing wrong with the car except that it's on fire.
Murray Walker, car-racing commentator

We threw our dice into the ring and it turned up trumps.
Bruce Rioch, on ITV

If you ever get the chance to visit Paris, do go up to the d'Orsay ... I love painters; they've got Monet, Ceganne and Déjà.
Tour de France commentator David Duffield ... or Monet, Cézanne and Degas

In some respects, I do this to provoke people. I like experiencing people's reactions. Some people may take my message to be "sod off" and others an offer of sex. I am very aware of people's reactions and love the fact that people recognize me as Lars Elstrup.

Soccer player Lars Elstrup explaining his arrest for exposing himself in a Copenhagen shopping center.

Alan Minter, boxer

Sure there have been injuries and deaths in boxing—but none of them serious.

I was watching the Blackburn game on TV on Sunday when it flashed on the screen that George (Ndah) had scored in the first minute at Birmingham. My first reaction was to call him up. Then I remembered he was out there playing.

Ade Akinbiyi, fellow soccer professional

I couldn't settle in Italy. It was like being in a foreign country.

Ian Rush, commenting on the difficulties of adjusting to playing soccer and living in a foreign country

Ah, isn't that nice? The wife of the Cambridge president is kissing the cox of the Oxford crew.
Harry Carpenter, commentating on the Oxford vs Cambridge Boat Race in 1977

Here we are in the Holy Land of Israel—a Mecca for tourists.

David Vine, BBC sports commentator, doing his bit to promote understanding of the geopolitical situation in the Middle East

Morcelli has the four fastest 1500-meter times ever, and all those times at 1500 meters.

David Coleman, sports commentator

. . . and later we will have action from the men's cockless pairs.
Sue Barker, former tennis player, now a sports commentator

Josepi Beloki, following in the footsteps of
Lance Indurain
Tour de France commentator David Duffield amalgamating six-times winner Lance Armstrong with five-times winner Miguel Indurain

Sex is an anti-climax after that!
Mark Fitzgerald, Grand National-winning jockey

These greens are so fast they must bikini-wax them.
Gary McCord, commenting on the pace of the golfing greens at Augusta

A sad ending, albeit a happy one.
Murray Walker, motorsports commentator

He has had seven **craps** as scrum-half for England.
The BBC's Jimmy Hill, handing over to a rugby commentator

Azinger is wearing an all-black outfit: black jumper, blue trousers, white shoes and a pink "tea-cosy" hat.
Golf commentator Renton Laidlaw, displaying 20–20 color vision

Street hockey is great for kids. It's energetic, competitive and skillful. And best of all it keeps them off the street.
Snippet from UK radio news report

[There are] fears that the balloon may be forced to ditch in the Pacific. Mr. Branson, however, remains buoyant and hopes to reach America.

Radio news item

A fascinating duel between three men.

David Coleman, sports commentator, describing the hammer-throwing event at the World Athletic Championship

Winfield goes back to the wall. He hits his head on the wall and it rolls off! It's rolling all the way back to second base! This is a terrible thing for the Padres!

Jerry Coleman, San Diego Padres announcer

The advantage of the rain is that if you have a quick bike, there's no advantage.

Barry Sheene, motorcycle legend

Greg Phillips

It was the fastest-ever swim over that distance on American soil.

THE LAW IS AN ASS

You were there until the time you left. Is that true?

Attorney's question to a witness in the courtroom

Question: What was the first thing your husband said to you when he woke up that morning?
Answer: He said, "Where am I, Cathy?"
Question: And why did that upset you?
Answer: My name is Susan.

Courtroom exchange between an attorney and a witness

Were you present when your picture was being taken?

Attorney's question to a witness

Now doctor, isn't it true that when a person dies in his sleep, he doesn't know about it until the next morning?
Question posed to a witness by an attorney, reported in the *Massachusetts Bar Association Lawyers' Journal*

Attorney: Doctor, before you performed the autopsy, did you check for a pulse?
Witness: No.
Attorney: Did you check for blood pressure?
Witness: No.
Attorney: Did you check for breathing?
Witness: No.
Attorney: So then, is it possible that the patient was alive when you began the autopsy?
Witness: No.
Attorney: How can you be so sure, Doctor?
Witness: Because his brain was sitting on my desk in a jar.
Attorney: But could the patient still have been alive, nevertheless?
Witness: It is possible that he could have been alive and practicing law somewhere.
Courtroom exchange between an attorney and a witness, as reported in the *Massachusetts Bar Association Lawyers' Journal*

Question: You say the stairs went down to the basement?
Answer: Yes.
Question: And these stairs, did they go up also?
Exchange between an attorney and a witness in the courtroom

Question: You went on a rather elaborate honeymoon, didn't you?
Answer: I went to Europe, sir.
Question: And you took your new wife?
Courtroom exchange between an attorney and a witness

How far apart were the vehicles at the time of the collision?
Question to a witness in the courtroom

Question: She had three children, right?
Answer: Yes.
Question: How many were boys?
Answer: None.
Question: Were there any girls?
Courtroom exchange between an attorney and a witness

Question: Were you acquainted with the deceased?
Answer: Yes, sir.
Question: Before or after he died?
Courtroom exchange between an attorney and a witness

Question: How was your first marriage terminated?
Answer: By death.
Question: And by whose death was it terminated?
Courtroom exchange between an attorney and a witness

The youngest son, the twenty-year-old, how **old** is he?
Question to a witness in the courtroom

For the purpose of this Part of this Schedule a person over pensionable age, not being an insured person, shall be treated as an employed person if he would be an insured person were he under pensionable age and would be an employed person were he an insured person.
UK National Insurance Act, 1964—
Schedule 1, Part II

Question: **Do you recall the time that you examined the body?**
Answer: **The autopsy started around 8:30 pm.**
Question: **And Mr. [name] was dead at the time?**
Answer: **No, he was sitting on the table wondering why I was doing an autopsy.**
Courtroom exchange between an attorney and an expert witness with a particularly dry sense of humor

Question: Can you describe the individual?
Answer: He was about medium height and had a beard.
Question: Was this a male or a female?
Courtroom exchange between an attorney and an expert witness

NON-PC WORLD

From now on we shall offer police jobs to qualified women regardless of sex.
Affirmative action statement on behalf of a town in the state of New Jersey

OSLO
ROME
PARIS

The only people who can't navigate instinctively are women and anyone trying to find Malpensa airport in Milan.
Jeremy Clarkson

Sensible and responsible women do not want to vote. The relative positions to be assumed by man and woman in the working out of our civilization were assigned long ago by a higher intelligence than ours.
Grover Cleveland, former US president, 1905

Rudyard Kipling

A woman is just a woman, but a good cigar is a smoke.

White folks was in caves while we was building empires...We taught philosophy and astrology and mathematics before Socrates and them Greek homos ever got around to it.

Rev. Al Sharpton, at Kean College, New Jersey in 1994 (speech transcribed in *The Forward*)

My wife bought me a patio heater for our wedding anniversary, and I've always been nervous about it. Now I know such things annoy Greenpeace, I shall keep it lit 24 hours a day.

Jeremy Clarkson

Antichrist! I renounce you and all your cults and creeds.

Rev. Ian Paisley interrupting Pope John Paul II in Strasbourg, while simultaneously unfurling a red banner that read "Pope John Paul II Anti-Christ"

Lord Denning, 1982

When a lady says no, she means perhaps. When she says perhaps, she means yes. But when she says yes she is no lady.

Human females like to drive massive four-wheel-drive cars; it suits their need to kill as many other road users as possible, damage other people's property, and if you believe David Cameron in his fair-trade sneakers, destroy the whole world as well.

Jeremy Clarkson

I ain't going to let no darkies and white folks segregate together in this town.

Eugene Connor, police commissioner of Birmingham, Alabama. Quoted in *The Observer* newspaper's "Sayings of the Week," March 1950

He is purple—the gay pride color—and his antenna is shaped like a triangle—the gay pride symbol.

Rev. Jerry Falwell, evangelist, "outs" *Teletubbies* character Tinky Winky in the February edition of the *National Liberty Journal* (edited and published by Falwell). On the *Today* show on NBC, Falwell also told Katie Couric that to have "little boys running around with purses and acting effeminate and leaving the idea that the masculine male, the feminine female is out, and gay is OK (is something) which Christians do not agree with"

Minorities, women, and the mentally-challenged are strongly advised to apply.
Job announcement from the Department of the Interior, National Biological Survey

There are only about 20 murders a year in London and not all are serious—some are just husbands killing their wives.
Commander G.H. Hatherill of Scotland Yard, February 1954

Rev. Jerry Falwell, evangelist

Most of these feminists are radical, frustrated lesbians, many of them, and man-haters, and failures in their relationships with men, and who have declared war on the male gender. The Biblical condemnation of feminism has to do with its radical philosophy and goals. That's the bottom line.

Harper's magazine, November 1853

Nothing could be more anti-biblical than letting women vote.

I thank heaven for a man like Adolf Hitler, who built a front line of defense against the anti-Christ of Communism.
Frank Buchman, US evangelist, August 1936

Pretty girls cost the same to employ as ugly ones. There's a shop in St James's Street, London, that sells lilac riding crops for £900. I have no use for anything like that but I buy one a week because the assistant is so pretty. In short, nobody likes to be served by a boot-faced old crow. Or, and this is for you, PC World, a man in a purple shirt.
Jeremy Clarkson

I believe that God created man. I object to teachers saying that we came from monkeys.

Ian Paisley, April 1980

Feminism encourages women to leave their husbands, kill their children, practice witchcraft, destroy capitalism and become lesbians.
Rev. Pat Robertson, speaking at the 1992 GOP Convention

Bad weather is like rape. If it's inevitable, just relax and enjoy it.
Clayton Williams, Republican, then running for the governorship of Texas. (Forced to account for the statement, which caused uproar, he said, "That was a joke . . . If anyone's offended, I apologize . . . This is not a Republican woman's club that we're having. It's a working cow camp—a tough world, where you get kicked in the testicles if you're not careful." Eventually, he had to cave in: "I apologize from the bottom of my heart")

Rev. Pat Robertson
If anyone understood what Hindus really believe, there would be no doubt that they have no business administering government policies.

All homosexuals should be castrated.
Evangelist Billy Graham (Graham later apologized for this statement)

Modern women defend their office with all the fierceness of domesticity. They fight for desk and typewriter as for the hearth and home, and develop a sort of wolfish wifehood on behalf of the invisible head of the firm. That is why they do office work so well; and that is why they ought not to do it.
Author G.K. Chesterton, writing in 1910

Chief Justice Moore, Alabama Supreme Court

Homosexual conduct is, and has been, considered abhorrent, immoral, detestable, a crime against nature, and a violation of the laws of nature and of nature's God upon which this nation and our laws are predicated. Such conduct violates both the criminal and civil laws of this State and is destructive to a basic building block of society—the family . . . It is an inherent evil against which children must be protected.

UFO Club, Hispanic Club . . .
Native American Club, Human Rights Club . . .
Young Democrats . . . UFO (Ultimate Frisbee Organization),
Advancement of Hispanic Students . . . Chinese Checkers Club . . .
HIS Club (Bible study club) . . . Latino Pride Club . . .
Students Against Drunk Driving. . . Students of the Orient . . .
Young Republicans.
Partial list of the high school clubs banned in 1996 by the Salt Lake City Board of Education in an attempt to crack down on gays and lesbians

Life in this society being, at best, an utter bore and no aspect of society being at all relevant to women, there remains to civic-minded, responsible, thrill-seeking females only to overthrow the government, eliminate the money system, institute complete automation, and destroy the male sex.
SCUM (Society for Cutting Up Men) manifesto—Valerie Solanos

Any nation is heathen that ain't strong enough to punch you in the jaw.

Will Rogers

The whole thing (the Women's Suffrage Movement) is an epidemic of vanity and restlessness—a disease as marked as measles or smallpox . . . Hereafter this outbreak will stand in history as an instance of national sickness, of moral decadence, of social disorder.
Mrs. Eliza Lynn Linton, US journalist, Partisans of the Wild Women, March 1892

Until now it has been thought that the level of testosterone in men is normal simply because they have it. But if you consider how abnormal their behavior is, then you are led to the hypothesis that almost all men are suffering from "testosterone poisoning."
From *A Feminist Dictionary*, eds. Kramarae and Treichler, (Pandora Press, 1985)

Woman's participation in political life . . .
would involve the domestic calamity of a
deserted home and the loss of the womanly
qualities for which refined men adore women
and marry them . . . Doctors tell us, too, that
thousands of children would be harmed or
killed before birth by the injurious effect of
untimely political excitement on their mothers.
Henry T. Finck, US critic, *The Independent*,
January 30, 1901

Josef Stalin

Those who cast the votes
decide nothing. Those who
count the votes decide
everything.

These eco-people are the
sort who were bullied at
school. They have poor dress
sense, limited social skills and
they know they stand little
chance of making much
headway in the world, so
they want it changed.
Jeremy Clarkson

MEN VERSUS WOMEN

Heterosexual intercourse is the pure, formalized expression of contempt for women's bodies.
Andrea Dworkin

Rod Stewart, incurable romantic

I've always been the one to push and shove and say, "Sorry, that's it darlin', it's all over, goodbye. Take twenty Valium and have a stomach pump and that's the end of it."

I've tried several varieties of sex. The conventional position makes me claustrophobic and the others give me a stiff neck or lockjaw.
Tallulah Bankhead, actress, 1972

Men are propelled by genetically ordained impulses over which they have no control, to distribute their seed into as many females as possible.
Marlon Brando, 1994

Philip Marlowe

A woman will lie about anything, just to stay in practice.

The male chromosome is an incomplete female chromosome. In other words, the male is a walking abortion; aborted at the gene stage. To be male is to be deficient, emotionally limited; maleness is a deficiency disease and males are emotional cripples.
Valerie Solanos

You can't stay married in a situation where you are afraid to go to sleep in case your wife might cut your throat.

Mike Tyson

Women are like elephants to me: nice to look at, but I wouldn't want to own one.
W.C. Fields

My notion of a wife at 40 is that a man should be able to change her, like a banknote, for two 20s.
Warren Beatty, 1997

How many husbands have I had? You mean apart from my own?
Zsa Zsa Gabor

I suppose when they reach a certain age some men are afraid to grow up. It seems the older the men get, the younger their new wives get.
Elizabeth Taylor

A bachelor's life is no life for a single man.
Samuel Goldwyn

I wish men had boobs because I like the feel of them. It's so funny—when I record I sing with a hand over each of them. Maybe it's a comfort thing.
Baby Spice (Emma Bunton) of the Spice Girls.

Marriage is a great institution.
Elizabeth Taylor

He's probably the world's most beautiful looking man, yet he doesn't think he's that gorgeous. And to me he's just **smelly**, farty Leo.
Kate Winslet talking about Leonardo Di Caprio

His previous wives just didn't understand him.

Jan Chamberlain, wife Number 8 for Mickey Rooney

My mother says I didn't open my eyes for 8 days after I was born, but when I did, the first thing I saw was an engagement ring. I was hooked.
Elizabeth Taylor

Cindy Crawford, supermodel

Models are like baseball players. We make a lot of money quickly, but all of a sudden we're 30 years old, we don't have a college education, we're qualified for nothing and we're used to a very nice lifestyle. The best thing is to marry a movie star.

Some of my best leading men have been dogs and horses.
Elizabeth Taylor

Maurice Chevalier

Many a man has fallen in love with a girl in a light so dim he would not have chosen a suit by it.

Love is like playing checkers. You have to know which man to move.
Moms Mabley

Men have always detested women's gossip because they suspect the truth: their measurements are being taken and compared.
Erica Jong

Men are gentle, honest and straightforward. Women are convoluted, deceptive and dangerous.
Erin Pizzey

The more I know about men the more I like dogs.
Gloria Allred

On the one hand, we'll never experience childbirth. On the other hand, we can open all our own jars.

Bruce Willis

Bachelors have consciences, married men have wives.
H. L. Mencken

Why one man rather than another? It was odd. You find yourself involved with a fellow for life just because he was the one that you met when you were nineteen.
Simone De Beauvoir

When two people decide to get a divorce, it isn't a sign that they "don't understand" one another, but a sign that they have, at last, begun to.
Helen Rowland

I would rather be a beggar and single than a queen and married.
Elizabeth I of England

A married couple are well suited when both partners usually feel the need for a quarrel at the same time.
Jean Rostand

HISTORY IS BUNK!

Lord Uxbridge: I've lost my leg, by God!
Wellington: By God, sir, so you have!
Exchange at the Battle of Waterloo, June 18, 1815

Germans who wish to use firearms should join the SS or the SA—ordinary citizens don't need guns, as their having guns doesn't serve the State.
Heinrich Himmler

Merde!
The famous (excretory) exclamation from Major General Pierre Cambronne, Napoleon's great military leader, moments before his capture at the Battle of Waterloo, 1815. (It became known as "le mot de Cambronne" (the word of Cambronne)

I wouldn't believe Hitler was dead even if he told me so himself.
The Führer's Central Bank Governor, May 1945

Adolf Eichmann, January 1961

I was an expert on migration problems.

I still believe I have a mission to carry out to the end, and I intend to carry it out to the end without giving up my throne. I'm convinced the monarchy in Iran will last longer than your regimes.

The (then) Shah of Iran in October 1973

I hope that what I have said today will at least make television, radio and the press first recognize the great responsibility they have to report all the news and, second, recognize that they have a right and a responsibility, if they're against a candidate, to give him the shaft, but also recognize if they give him the shaft, put one lonely reporter on the campaign who will report what the candidate says now and then. Thank you gentlemen, and good day.

Richard Nixon bidding farewell to the press after his failed bid for the governorship of California in November 1962.
["You won't have Nixon to kick around any more, gentlemen. This is my last press conference"]

Without censorship, things can get terribly confused in the public mind.

General William Westmoreland, during the war in Vietnam

Writing about the Nixon Administration is about as exciting as covering the Prudential Life Insurance Company.

Art Buchwald, July 1970

I do not believe in the probability of anything very much worse than mustard gas being produced.

Professor J.B.S. Haldane, 1937

The best defense against the atom bomb is not to be there when it goes off.

The British Army Journal, February 1949

The US must be willing to continue bombing until every work of man in North Vietnam is gone.
General Curtis Le May, October 1968

General Smuts, May 1917

I have often said to myself that the history of South Africa is the one true and great romance of modern history.

I do not know how many we shot . . . It all started when hordes of natives surrounded the police station.
If they do these things they must learn their lesson the hard way.
Colonel Pienaar, Area Police Commander, speaking after the Sharpeville massacre in South Africa, March 1960

Much of the trouble in Russia, politics apart, is due, I believe, to the fact that Russia is not a games-playing nation.

W.W. Wakefield, March 1928

Josef Stalin

One death is a tragedy; a million deaths is a statistic.

Drill for oil? You mean drill into the ground to try and find oil? You're crazy.

Workers whom Edwin L. Drake tried to enlist to his project to drill for oil in 1859

If the British attack our cities we will simply erase theirs. The hour will come when one of us will break up, and it won't be Nazi Germany.

Adolf Hitler, September 1940

To save the town, it became necessary to destroy it.

US officer, speaking in 1968 of an "incident" in the Vietnam War

Let them eat cake.

Marie Antoinette—she meant "brioche," a sugary type of bread, but the comment nonetheless displayed her appalling ignorance of the famine and poverty then ravaging France, and further incited the mob against the royal pair

The most significant fact of modern history is that America speaks English.

Ludwig von Bismarck

We have stopped losing the war in Vietnam.

Robert McNamara, US Defense Secretary, *The Observer* "Sayings of the Week," December 1965

I don't see much future for the Americans . . . Everything about the behavior of American Society reveals that it's half-Judaized, and the other half negrified. How can one expect a state like that to hold together?
Adolf Hitler, quoted in *Hitler's Table Talk* (1953)

Josef Stalin, November 1935

Gaiety is the most outstanding feature of the Soviet Union.

All those who are not racially pure are mere chaff.

Adolf Hitler, in *Mein Kampf*

After the war, there will be a revolution in the United States, and presumably elsewhere, coming at a time of profound economic dislocation.

Leon Trotsky, in 1940

I tell you that Wellington is a bad general, that the English are bad troops, and that this affair is only a *déjeuner*.

Attributed to Napoleon I on the morning of Waterloo, June 18, 1815

The whole nation loves him, because it feels safe in his hands, like a child in the arms of his mother.

Dr. Joseph Goebbels, speaking of the German Chancellor, Adolf hitler, in 1934

A third-rate burglary attempt not worthy of further White House comment.

Ron Ziegler, White House press spokesman, on the Watergate break-in, June 1972

It was very successful, but it fell on the wrong planet.

Comment attributed to the German rocket engineer Werner von Braun, referring to the first V2 rocket (which he designed) to hit London during World War II

Being a lady war correspondent is like being a lady wrestler—you can be one of them at a time, but not both simultaneously.
Dickey Chapelle, speaking at Danang, November 2, 1965. (Ms. Chapelle was killed in action the following day)

The situation is splendid. God willing, we are going forward to great and victorious days.

Kaiser Wilhelm, June 1918

I cannot conceive of any condition which would cause a ship to founder. I cannot conceive of any vital disaster happening to a vessel. Modern shipbuilding has gone beyond that.

E.J. Smith, of the White Star Line, future captain of the *Titanic*

You will give England the most certain death stroke . . . We shall succeed in our enterprises . . . The fates are with us.
Napoleon, rallying his troops before the Battle of Waterloo, 1815

It's only a toy.

Gardiner Greene Hubbard, co-founder of the National Geographic Society and inventor Alexander Graham Bell's future father-in-law, upon seeing Bell's newfangled "telephone" in 1876

This morning I had another talk with the German Chancellor, Herr Hitler, and here is the paper which bears his name upon it as well as mine . . . "We regard the agreement signed last night, and the Anglo-German Naval Agreement, as symbolic of the desire of our two peoples never to go to war with one another again."

Prime Minister Neville Chamberlain, speaking to reporters at Heston Airport, September 30, 1938, on his return from a second visit to Hitler, during which the Munich Agreement was signed

I cannot see any nation or combination of nations producing the money necessary to put up a satellite in outer space or to circumnavigate the moon.

Sir Richard Woolley, Astronomer Royal, in 1957 (or, as he put it on another occasion, "Space travel is utter bilge")

Remember, the German people are the chosen of God. On me, the German Emperor, the spirit of God has descended. I am His sword, His weapon, and His vice-regent.

Kaiser Wilhelm, August 4, 1914

I feel very proud, even though they didn't elect me, to be president of the Argentines.

General Galtieri, 1982

I often think how much easier the world would have been to manage if Herr Hitler and Signor Mussolini had been to Oxford.

Lord Halifax, November 1937

...this monkey mythology of Darwin is the cause of permissiveness, promiscuity, prophylactics, perversions, pregnancies, abortions, pornotherapy, pollution, poisoning and proliferation of crimes of all types.

Judge Braswell Dean

Ian Smith, March 1976

I don't believe in black majority rule in Rhodesia . . . not in a thousand years.

The airship probably has many years of life—perhaps at least fifty.
Sir Sefton Brancker, designer of the airship R101, which crashed at Beauvais in France on its maiden flight in 1930—killing, among others, its inventor

[Professor Goddard] does not know the relation between action and reaction and the need to have something better than a vacuum against which to react . . . He seems to lack the basic knowledge ladled out daily in high schools.
The New York Times (1921), in an editorial discussing Robert Goddard's revolutionary rocket work

Hurrah, boys! We've got them. We'll finish them up and then go home to our station.

General George Custer, before the battle with the Native Americans in the Valley of the Little Big Horn, 1876

I must confess that my imagination, in spite even of spurring, refuses to see any sort of submarine doing anything except suffocating its crew and floundering at sea.

H.G. Wells—author of *The Time Machine* and *War of the Worlds*— in 1902

I see no good reasons why the views given in this volume should shock the religious sensibilities of anyone.

Charles Darwin, in a preamble to his seminal work on evolution, *The Origin of Species*, which contradicted the creationists' vision and turned Victorian society upside down

Nothing is gained by exaggerating the possibilities of tomorrow. We need not worry about the consequences of breaking up the atom.

Floyd W. Parsons, engineer, in the *Saturday Evening Post*, 1931

Where a calculator on the ENIAC is equipped with 18,000 vacuum tubes and weighs 30 tons, computers in the future may have only 1,000 vacuum tubes and weigh only 1.5 tons.

Extract from the journal *Popular Mechanics*, March 1949

Anybody can make a mistake.

Italian doctor representing a small religious cult who had shut themselves in a cabin on Mont Blanc, believing the end of the world would come about . . . at 1:45 p.m. The doctor was speaking (sheepishly) at 1:56 p.m, July 1959

It can be exploited for a certain time as a scientific curiosity, but apart from that it has no commercial value whatsoever.
August Lumière on his invention, the moving picture projector

Ours has been the first, and doubtless to be the last, to visit this profitless locality.
Lt. Joseph Ives, after visiting the Grand Canyon in 1861

Very interesting, Whittle, my boy, but it will never work.
Cambridge University Aeronautical Engineering Department's response to Frank Whittle, after viewing his pioneering designs for the jet engine

It possesses many advantages over morphine . . . It is not hypnotic and there is no danger of acquiring the habit.
James R.L. Daly's analysis of a new drug, diacetylmorphine—a.k.a. heroin—in the *Boston Medical and Surgical Journal* of 1900

No one knows more about this mountain than Harry. And it don't dare blow up on him!

Harry Truman (not the US president), owner of a mountain cabin near Mount St. Helens. The inactive —or so he thought—volcano blew up a few days later, engulfing it and its owner

As you may well know, Mr President, "railroad" carriages are pulled at the enormous speed of 15 miles per hour by "engines" which, in addition to endangering life and limb of passengers, roar and snort their way through the countryside, setting fire to crops, scaring the livestock and frightening women and children. The Almighty certainly never intended that people should travel at such breakneck speed.

Martin Van Buren, then governor of New York, in a letter to President Andrew Jackson, 1829

The most ambitious United States endeavor in the years ahead will be the campaign to land men on neighboring Mars. Most experts estimate the task can be accomplished by 1985.
Extract from the *Wall Street Journal*, 1966

This plane is the greatest single step forward in combat aircraft in several decades.
Robert McNamara, then US Secretary of Defense, announcing the revolutionary F-111 in 1964 (the aircraft then rewarded his confidence by dropping out of the sky with disconcerting regularity)

A pretty mechanical toy.

Lord Kitchener, British Secretary of State for war, c.1917 dismissing the tank as a weapon of war

DUBBYA

Laura and I really don't realize how bright our children is sometimes until we get an objective analysis.
George W. Bush, *Meet the Press*, April 15, 2000

I have opinions of my own—strong opinions—but I don't always agree with them.

George W. Bush

What's not fine is, rarely is the question asked: Is our children learning?
George W. Bush, January 14, 2000

You're free. And freedom is beautiful. And, you know, it'll take time to restore chaos and order—order out of chaos. But we will.

George W. Bush, Washington DC, April 13, 2003

When I was young and irresponsible, I was young and irresponsible.
George W. Bush

Redefining the role of the United States from enablers to keep the peace to enablers to keep the peace from peacekeepers is going to be an assignment.
George W. Bush

I know how hard it is for you to put food on your family.
George W. Bush, talking about putting food on the plates of youngsters, in Greater Nashua, New Hampshire, January 27, 2000

I've changed my style somewhat, as you know. I'm less . . . I pontificate less, although it may be hard to tell it from this show. And I'm more interacting with people.
George W. Bush, *Meet The Press*, NBC, February 13, 2000

The **fact** that he relies on **facts**—says things that are **not** factual—are going to undermine his campaign.
George W. Bush, on Al Gore, quoted in *The New York Times*, March 4, 2000

This is a world that is much more uncertain than the past. In the past we were certain, we were certain it was us versus the Russians in the past. We were certain, and therefore we had huge nuclear arsenals aimed at each other to keep the peace . . . You see, even though it's an uncertain world, we're certain of some things.
George W. Bush

The senator (McCain) has got to understand if he's going to have—he can't have it both ways. He can't take the high **horse** and then claim the low road.

George W. Bush to reporters in Florence, South Carolina, about his Republican nomination opponent, February 17, 2000

Keep good relations with the Grecians.

George W. Bush quoted in *The Economist*, June 12, 1999

The problem with the French is that they don't have a word for **entrepreneur.**

George W. Bush's aside to British Prime Minister Tony Blair during a conference attended by French President Jacques Chirac; the discussion was economics and, in particular, the decline of the French economy

George W. Bush: I was not elected to serve one party.
Jon Stewart: You were not elected.
George W. Bush: I have something else to ask you, to ask every American. I ask you to pray for this great nation.
Jon Stewart: We're way ahead of you.
Exchange on *The Daily Show*

I was raised in the West. The West of Texas. It's pretty close to California. In more ways than Washington DC is close to California.

George W. Bush, quoted in the *Los Angeles Times*, April 8, 2000

If you're sick and tired of the politics of cynicism and polls and principles, come and join this campaign.

George W. Bush, Hilton Head, South Carolina, February 16, 2000

I think anybody who doesn't think I'm smart enough to handle this job is underestimating. George W. Bush on his ability to head the world's superpower

The American people's expectations are that we will fail. Our mission is to exceed their expectations.

George W. Bush at one of his first televised cabinet meetings in an opening speech to the cabinet

First I'd like to spank all the teachers . . .

George W. Bush, in an address to American teachers on NBC. (A short pause followed, during which a flicker of recognition passed over his face as his mistake dawned. Then he continued with his speech)

Bush: First of all, *Cinco de Mayo* is not the independence day. That's *Dieciséis de Septiembre*, and . . .
Interviewer: What's that in English?
Bush: Fifteenth of September.
Exchange between Bush and interviewer on *Hardball* on MSNBC, May 31, 2000
(*Dieciséis de Septiembre* is September 16 . . .)

Neither in French nor in English nor in **Mexican**.

George W. Bush at the Summit of the Americas in Quebec City, when asked to answer questions about what had taken place.

And America needs a military where our **breast** and brightest are proud to serve, and proud to stay.

George W. Bush's remark to the troops of Fort Stewart, Georgia

We cannot let terrorists and rogue nations hold this nation hostile or hold our allies hostile.

George W. Bush on the matter of US national security, August 21, 2000

Education is my top priority. However, education is not my top priority.

George W. Bush

It's clearly a budget.
It's got a lot of numbers in it.

George W. Bush, *Reuters*, 5 May 2000

We'll let the other countries of the world be the peacekeepers and the great country called America be the pacemakers.
George W. Bush

George W. Bush to UK Prime Minister Tony Blair at the G8 summit in July 2006

Yo, Blair. How are you doing?

I am mindful not only of preserving executive powers for myself, but for predecessors as well.
George W. Bush

There's an old saying in Tennessee—I know it's in Texas, probably in Tennessee...that says, fool me once, shame on...shame on you. Fool me...you can't get fooled again.
George W. Bush

Well, I think if you say you're going to do something and don't do it, that's trustworthiness.
George W. Bush

George W. Bush, at the Gridiron dinner

A hobby I enjoy is mapping the human genome. I hope one day I can clone another Dick Cheney. Then I won't have to do anything.

No, I eat three square meals a day.
George W. Bush's response to a reporter who asked if he was dyslexic

Putting "subliminable" [sub-lim-in-a-bal] messages into commercials is absurd.
George W. Bush, countering claims that he put subliminal messages in a commercial

I understand small business growth. I was one.
George W. Bush, quoted in *New York Daily News*, February 19, 2000

I don't think anybody anticipated the breach of the levees.
George W. Bush on *Good Morning America*, speaking on Hurricane Katrina and the flooding of New Orleans, September 1, 2005

It is clear our nation is reliant upon big foreign oil. More and more of our imports come from overseas.
George W. Bush, September 2000

Our enemies are innovative and resourceful, and so are we. They never stop thinking about new ways to harm our country and our people, and neither do we.
Washington DC, August 5, 2004

I think they have misunderestimated me.

George W. Bush's response to the question, "What do you think of citizens saying you are too religious?" in *People* magazine

For a century and a half now, America and Japan have formed one of the great and enduring alliances of modern times.
Tokyo, February 18, 2002

Free societies are hopeful societies. And free societies will be allies against these hateful few who have no conscience, who kill at the whim of a hat.
George W. Bush, Washington DC, September 17, 2004

GOING CRITICAL

God may have created the world in six days, but while he was resting on the seventh, Beelzebub popped up and did this place.
Jeremy Clarkson writing about Detroit

It's like swimming in undiluted sewage.
Prince Charles emerging from the surf at St. Kilda Beach, near Melbourne. The comment caused a storm in Australia (Charles deserved "a good thump under the ear," according to one local mayor)

A 'classic' is something that everybody wants to have read and nobody wants to read.
Mark Twain

One must have a heart of stone to read the death of Little Nell without laughing.
Oscar Wilde on Dickens' *The Old Curiosity Shop*

Jeremy Clarkson

A Range Rover, doing 10,000 miles a year, produces less pollution a day than a cow **farting**.

The not noticeably Greek Christian Bale is so wooden he seems intent on a one-man impersonation of Epping Forest.
Christopher Tookey on *Captain Corelli's Mandolin*, *Daily Mail*

This girl is all underdog and she's got a real scene-stealing dog besides. The dog's soulful expressions have more depth than anything else in the picture.
Pauline Kael on *Flashdance*, *The New Yorker* 1983

Telling people at a dinner party you drive a Nissan Almera is like telling them you've got the ebola virus and you're about to sneeze.
Jeremy Clarkson

I cannot conceive of how empty, pointless and lacking in ambition or style your life must be for the (Kia) Sedona to be a solution. It is like alcohol-free beer, a pointless car-free facsimile of the real thing, and as a result, it can have no place in the life of a sentient being.
Clarkson's Cars of the Year 2008, *Times Online*

. . . comes off as being no better than a mannered version of *The Amityville Horror*."
Danny Peary,
describing *The Shining* for *Film Fanatic*

This is a Renault Espace,
probably the best of the people carriers.
Not that that's much to shout about. That's
like saying 'Oh good, I've got syphilis, the best
of the sexually transmitted diseases!'
Jeremy Clarkson

I'd rather go to work on my
hands and knees than drive
there in a Ford Galaxy.
Whoever designed the Ford
Galaxy upholstery had a
cauliflower fixation.
I would rather have a
vasectomy than buy a
Ford Galaxy.
Jeremy Clarkson

**I think the problem is that it's French...
It's a surrender monkey.**
Jeremy Clarkson talking about the
Renault Clio V6.

The
only person who
looked good in a 4-seater
convertible was Adolf Hitler
**Jeremy Clarkson on the Audi
RS4 Convertible**

**The entertainment value
is akin to watching war
newsreels while someone
shines a bright light in
your eye.**

Philip J. Kaplan on
Xanadu, 1983

**If you are clinically insane, by
which I mean you wake up in the
morning and you think you are an
onion, this is your car.**
Jeremy Clarkson on the BMW X3

Makes you long for something lighter and wittier such as a documentary on the Khmer Rouge.

Simon Rose on *Shanghai Surprise* 1986

I've seen **gangrenous** wounds better looking than this!
Jeremy Clarkson on the Porsche Cayenne

First the boring news: *Big Brother* is coming back for a second season. Now the ray of hope: CBS remodelled the house. The chicken coop is gone. They've booted the chickens. Nice touch. Those chickens were dragging down the show.
Rick Kushman on US *Big Brother*

Whenever I'm suffering from insomnia, I just look at a picture of a Toyota Camry and I'm straight off.
Jeremy Clarkson

You do not just avoid the Suzuki Wagon R.
You avoid it like you would avoid unprotected
sex with an Ethiopian transvestite.
Jeremy Clarkson

As something to live with
every day, I'd rather have bird flu.
In many ways this car is like herpes.
Great fun catching it but not so much fun
to live with every day.

**Jeremy Clarkson on the
Chevrolet Corvette Z06**

You can't get angry
at something this
stupefying; it seems
to have been made
by **trolls.**
Pauline Kael on *Song of
Norway*, 1970

Frank Rice,
Time

While much of the footage is
breathtaking, *Apocalypse Now* is
emotionally obtuse and
intellectually empty. It is not so
much an epic account of a grueling
war as an incongruous, extravagant
monument to artistic self-defeat.

I JUST WANT To THANK...

I just want to thank everyone I met in my entire life.
Kim Basinger, during her Oscar acceptance speech, March 1998

Elizabeth and I have been through too much to watch our marriage go up in flames. There is just too much love going for us ever to divorce.
Richard Burton, speaking amid rumors of troubles with his wife, Elizabeth Taylor, in 1974

I don't feel we did wrong in taking this great country away from them. There were great numbers of people who needed new land, and the Indians were selfishly trying to keep it for themselves.
John Wayne

Cher

They are **my tits** and if I wanna have them put on my back that is my own damn business.

I feel my best when I'm happy.
Winona Ryder

I loved Jordan. He was one of the greatest athletes of our time.
Mariah Carey, on the death of the King of Jordan

You can hardly tell where the computer models finish and the real dinosaurs begin.
Laura Dern, on the technical tricks employed in the film *Jurassic Park*

I can always judge people by the way they ring my doorbell.
Cynthia Payne, former London madam, October 1982

Celine Dion

To have your niece die in your arms is the greatest gift from God.

Beyond its entertainment value, *Baywatch* has enriched and, in many cases, helped save lives. I'm looking forward to the opportunity to continue with a project which has had such a significance for so many.
David Hasselhoff

Ich bin warm.

Sting, explaining to his audience at a German concert that he was feeling hot. To them, however, he was announcing, "I am gay"

Please forgive me! Is this really happening? Thank you so much. [Suddenly sobbing] Thank you so much! Oh my God! [Reading from autocue] "Please wrap up?" You have no idea how much I'm not wrapping up! Okay, gather. This is absolutely extraordinary, I've had an incredible couple of years. Thank you so much. Thank you so much! God! I'm so sorry Anne, Meryl, Kristin—oh God, who's the other one... Angelina!

Kate Winslet, 2009 Golden Globes

I don't know all the certain words to word it.

Vanilla Ice, on why he hired a ghostwriter for his autobiography

Nancy Reagan

I believe there would be people alive today if there were a death penalty.

My main hope for myself is to be where I am.

Woody Harrelson

Fiction writing is great. You can make up almost anything.
Ivana Trump, on her first novel

The only happy artist is a dead artist, because only then you can't change. After I die, I'll probably come back as a paintbrush.

Sylvester Stallone

There is certainly more in the future now than back in 1964.
Roger Daltrey of The Who

I'm learning English at the moment. I can say "Big Ben," "Hello Rodney," "Tower Bridge" and "loo."
Cher

My hairdresser calls me Beaujolais.
Victoria Beckham, referring to the British TV soap series *Footballers' Wives*, which featured a female character called "Chardonnay"

. . . sometimes like a grandfather clock, sometimes like an alarm clock, sometimes a cornucopian goddess, sometimes a curmudgeonly landlord, sometimes like the blossomiest blossom, sometimes a knot of seaweed, sometimes a storm, sometimes a cradle, sometimes the bees and the pollen, sometimes a dagger.
Actress Imogen Stubbs, on how she "feels as a mother," *Daily Telegraph*

I can't deny the fact you like me. Right now, you like me.
Sally Field, gushing in her acceptance of the Oscar for Best Actress in 1984 for the film *Places in the Heart*

Claudia Schiffer

I've looked in the mirror every day for twenty years.
It's the same face.

I would not have been able to play this role had I not understood **love** with a tremendous magnitude.
Gwyneth Paltrow, expressing her enormous gratitude to all concerned and sobbing uncontrollably as she accepted the Oscar for Best Actress in 1998, for her performance in *Shakespeare in Love*

**We'll be together forever.
We are like twins.**
Britt Ekland, of her new
boyfriend Rod Stewart
(in 1976)

Alicia
Silverstone

I think that *Clueless* was very deep.
I think it was deep in the way that it
was very light. I think lightness has
to come from a very deep place if
it's true lightness.

My body is in tumult . . .
I would like to be . . .
lying down and making
love to everybody.

Christina
Aguilera

Roberto Benigni, the double Oscar
winner of 1998 (for Best Actor and
Best Foreign Film) in his
acceptance speech—in broken
English—for his film *Life is
Beautiful*. He later added, "I am so
happy, I want to wag my tail"

So where's the
Cannes film
festival being
held this year?

I went in and said, "If I see one more
gratuitous shot of a woman's body, I'm
quitting . . ." I think the show should be
emotional storylines, morals, real-life
heroes. And that's what we're doing.
David Hasselhoff, explaining the new, highbrow
angle in beach-babe TV series *Baywatch*

I want to take this opportunity to say how proud I am of my little brother, my dear, sweet, talented brother. Just imagine what you could accomplish if you tried celibacy.
Shirley Maclaine, presenting an Oscar to her (not amused) brother Warren Beatty for *Reds* in 1981

I personally believe that US Americans are unable to do so because, uh, some, people out there in our nation don't have maps and, uh, I believe that our, uh, education like such as, uh, South Africa and, uh, the Iraq, everywhere like such as, and, I believe that they should, our education over here in the US should help the US, uh, or, uh, should help South Africa and should help the Iraq and the Asian countries, so we will be able to build up our future, for our (children).
Caitlin Upton, Miss Teen South Carolina answering the question: Why can't a fifth of Americans find the USA on a world map? It became a YouTube classic

Linda Evangelista, supermodel

I don't wake up for less than $10,000 a day.

Superficiality and vulgarity, especially in women.
Nancy Reagan, owning up to her pet peeves in December 1981

You mean like a book?

Justin Timberlake when asked during a *Rolling Stone* interview what was the best thing he had read all year

I am a really big Elvis fan and I think the reason why we did the whole Elvis thing is because, you know, he's from Vegas.
Britney Spears (Elvis was actually from Tupelo, Mississippi; and moved to Memphis)

Britney Spears

I like most of the places I've been to, but I've never really wanted to go to Japan, simply because I don't like eating fish, and I know that's very popular out there in Africa.

I really am a cat transformed into a woman.
Brigitte Bardot, quoted by Tony Crawley in, *Bébé: The Films of Brigitte Bardot*

I would like to spank director Spike Jonze.

Meryl Streep, misreading a faxed acceptance speech at the 2003 Bafta Awards

I would not live forever, because we should not live forever, because if we were supposed to live forever, then we would live forever, but we cannot live forever, which is why I would not live forever.

Miss Alabama in the 1994 *Miss USA* contest. This was her answer to the question, "'If you could live forever, would you and why?"

Mick Jagger in 1970

I'd rather be dead than singing *Satisfaction* when I'm 45.

For twenty years I was cornered and hounded like an animal. I didn't throw myself off my balcony only because I knew people would photograph me lying dead.
Brigitte Bardot

It's so bad being homeless in winter. They should buy a plane ticket and go somewhere hot like the Caribbean where they can eat free fish all day.
Lady Victoria Hervey, the so-called "It girl" (reportedly overheard remark)

I don't need the security of marriage. What I need is a romantic attachment.
***Playboy* boss Hugh Hefner, then aged 75**

Al Capone

You can get much further with a kind word and a gun than you can with just a kind word.

As I said to the Queen, I can't stand name-droppers.

TV presenter, Alan Whicker

Where the hell is **Australia** anyway?
Britney Spears

I suppose a knighthood is out of the question now?
Spike Mulligan in a telegram to Prince Charles, after calling the prince a "little groveling bastard"; Mulligan later received an honorary knighthood

Isn't Halle Berry the most beautiful woman? I have a film I'd like to be in her with. I mean, I'd like to be with her in.
Ewan McGregor, actor, to an interviewer at the 2002 Golden Globe Awards

I know nothing about nothing.
Former Playmate and TV presenter Anna Nicole Smith

I would like to be an archaeologist.
Mike Tyson, on his career options beyond the world of boxing

I will feel equality has arrived when we can elect to office women who are as incompetent as some of the men who are already there.

Maureen Reagan, daughter of President Reagan, in 1982

I've learned not to put things in my mouth that are bad for me.

Monica Lewinsky on CNN's *Larry King Live*. They were discussing her weight loss through the Jenny Craig program. Her phrasing, it seems, was perfectly innocent

(Wonderful) to be on terracotta again.

Laura Corrigan, announcing her pleasure at being back on terra firma after disembarking from the yacht on which she had been cruising

Smoking kills. If you're killed, you've lost a very important part of your life.

Brooke Shields, offering up her nugget of truth during a national *No Smoking* campaign in the US

I resign in Florida.

Backstreet Boys' singer Nick Carter. The comment fooled the interviewer—and Carter's fellow band members—into thinking he was leaving the group

Richard Gere

I know who I am. No one else knows who I am. If I was a giraffe and somebody said I was a snake I'd think, "No, actually I am a giraffe."

The band never actually split up— we just stopped speaking to each other and went our own separate ways. **Boy George, talking about Culture Club on BBC Radio 2**

Changing someone's life is not the best, it is not wanting to change the other life. It is being who you are that changes another's life. Do you understand? Juliette Binoche, French actress

I'm the Hiroshima of love. Sylvester Stallone

Cystitis is a living death, it really is. Nobody ever talks about it, but if I was faced with a choice between having my **arms removed** and getting cystitis, I'd wave goodbye to my arms quite happily. Louise Wener of rock band Sleeper, in *Q magazine*

(*Dances With Wolves*) is a bonding film for all. You could put it anywhere in history— the Berlin Wall, Kuwait.

Kevin Costner

I loved making *Rising Sun*. I got into the psychology of why she liked to get strangled and tied up in plastic bags. It has to do with low self-esteem.
Tatjana Patitz on her role in the film *Rising Sun*

I get to go to a lot of famous places, like Canada.
Britney Spears on the good bits of being famous

I think *Baywatch* is such a hit here (the UK) because of the weather.
Actress Gena Lee Nolin (nothing to do with the bronzed beach-babes, then)

David Hasselhoff

Anyone who makes fun of *Baywatch* is doing it out of ignorance.

It's not that I dislike many people. It's just that I don't like many people.
Bryant Gumbel, TV newscaster

In an action film you act in the action. If it's a dramatic film you act in the drama.
Jean-Claude Van Damme, action hero, explaining the actor's craft

Warren Beatty

Charity is taking an ugly girl to lunch.

I think a man can have two, maybe three affairs, while he is married. But three is the absolute maximum. After that, you're cheating.
Yves Montand, French actor who hasn't read his Ten Commandments properly

Playboy isn't like the downscale, male bonding, beer-swilling phenomenon that is being promoted now. My whole notion was the romantic connection between male and female.
Hugh Hefner

Jeremy Irons, English actor

I act from my crotch. That's where my force is.

I was asked to come to Chicago because Chicago is one of our fifty-two states.
Raquel Welch, speaking on *Larry King Live*

It's a good way to get rid of a few nuts, you know. You gotta look at it that way.
Ted Turner, TV mogul, looking on the bright side of the Heaven's Gate Cult mass suicide

Donna Summer, singer

God had to create disco music so that I could be born and be successful.

At the risk of sounding pompous, I guess I would align it (playing with Tin Machine in 1991) with deconstructionism. The point made by the French in the Sixties that we are working our way towards a society that is deeply involved with hybridization and contradictory information almost to the point where contradiction simply ceases to exist.
David Bowie, taking the risk he refers to—and running all the way with it

It seemed that my wife Shirley was always pregnant until we found out what was causing it.

Pat Boone, singer, explaining why his wife hadn't accompanied him on trips previously

There are many dying children out there whose last wish is to meet me.

David Hasselhoff

There aren't enough men to go around . . . Every time there's a plane accident, it's one hundred men dead . . . and I literally think, "Why couldn't some women have been on that flight?"

Helen Gurley Brown, *Cosmopolitan* editor and author of *Sex and the Single Girl*

If you have intercourse you run the risk of dying and the ramifications of death are final.

Cyndi Lauper, singer

Cher

I'm still friends with all my exes, apart from my husbands.

SOUNDBITES BACK

Tony Blair

Now is not the time for soundbites. I can feel the hand of history on my shoulder.

Politics gives guys so much power that they tend to behave badly around women. I hope I never get into that.
A pre-Monica Lewinsky Bill Clinton

Once you've seen one ghetto, you've seen them all.
Spiro T. Agnew, Vice-President under Nixon

That's not a lie, it's a terminological inexactitude.
Alexander Haig, US Secretary of State

I regret to say that we of the FBI are powerless to act in cases of oral-genital intimacy, unless it has in some way obstructed interstate commerce.
J. Edgar Hoover, former FBI Director

> Sure there are dishonest men in local government. But there are dishonest men in national government too.
> **Richard Nixon**

We lead in exporting jobs.

Dan Quayle, addressing the Chamber of Commerce of Evansville, Indiana (where three large companies had been sent to the wall in the previous four years). He corrected himself, substituting the word "products" for "jobs"

I got tired listening to one million dollars here, one million dollars there. It's so petty.
Imelda Marcos, former First Lady of the Philippines and world-renowned shoe collector

H. L. Mencken

Democracy is the art and science of running the circus from the monkey cage.

I have said that I'm not running and I'm having a great time being Pres— being a first-term senator.

Hillary Clinton, on whether she had any presidential ambitions

I'm praying, of course, that Hillary will win. If she doesn't—Lord, I'll have to call Revlon again.
Vernon Jordan, friend and advisor to Bill Clinton, on Hillary's New York State bid. (Jordan was criticized during the Clinton impeachment trial for having called Revlon to secure Monica Lewinsky a job)

The only way the French are going in is if we tell them we found truffles in Iraq.
Dennis Miller, on France's refusal to back the US-led invasion of Iraq in 2003

James Bond is a man of honor, a symbol of real value to the free world.
Ronald Reagan

Lyndon B. Johnson

I never trust a man unless I've got his pecker in my pocket.

Last time I saw (Clinton) he was swinging on the chandelier in the Oval Office with a brassiere around his head, Viagra in one hand and a Bible in the other, and he was torn between good and evil.
Congressman James A. Traficant, Jr. (Democrat, Ohio)

Walter Mondale (Democratic candidate): George Bush doesn't have the manhood to apologize.

George H.W. Bush (Republican candidate): Well, on the manhood thing, **I'll put mine up against his any time.**

I am honored today to begin my first term as the governor of Baltimore—that is, Maryland.
William Donald Schaefer, in his inaugural address

We have, of course, often done it before, but never on a pavement outside a hotel in Eastbourne. We have done it in various rooms in one way or another at various functions. It is perfectly genuine—and normal and right—so to do.
William Whitelaw (on kissing Margaret Thatcher) in 1975

This President is going to lead us out of this recovery. It will happen.
Vice-President Dan Quayle at a campaign stop

Freedom's untidy.

Donald Rumsfeld, US Defense Secretary, on looting in Baghdad following the US-led invasion of Iraq in 2003

The President has kept all of the promises he intended to keep.
George Stephanopolous, Clinton aide, speaking on *Larry King Live*

Cheese-eating surrender monkeys.
Donald Rumsfeld, US Defense Secretary, describing the French

Dan Quayle

Rural Americans are real Americans. There's no doubt about that. You can't always be sure with other Americans. Not all of them are real.

I haven't committed a crime. What I did was fail to comply with the law.
David Dinkins, former mayor of New York City, defending himself against accusations that he had failed to pay his taxes

When my sister and I were growing up, there was never any doubt in our minds that men and women were equal, if not more so.
Al Gore, to an audience composed mostly of women

I was recently on a tour of Latin America, and the only regret I have was that I didn't study Latin harder in school so I could converse with those people.
Dan Quayle

My friends, no matter how rough the road may be, we can and we will never, never surrender to what is right.

Dan Quayle, speaking to the Christian Coalition about the need for sexual abstinence if AIDS is to be curbed

I will have a foreign-handed foreign policy.

George W. Bush

Polacks.

Spiro T. Agnew, on Polish-Americans, 1968

For seven and a half years I've worked alongside President Reagan. We've had triumphs. Made some mistakes. We've had some sex . . . uh, setbacks.
George H. W. Bush

You can tell a lot about a fellow's character by the way he eats jelly beans.

President Reagan, January 1981

Gerald R. Ford, US President

If Lincoln was alive today, he'd roll over in his grave.

The American people would not want to know of any misquotes that Dan Quayle may or may not make.

Dan Quayle

The caribou love it. They rub against it and they have babies. There are more caribou in Alaska than you can shake a stick at.

George H. W. Bush, on the Alaska pipeline

I'm not against the blacks and a lot of the good blacks will attest to that.

Evan Mecham, then Governor of Arizona

I strongly support the feeding of children.

President Gerald R. Ford, stating the obvious when commenting on the school lunch program

> Although in public I refer to him as Mr. Vice-President, in private I call him George . . . When I talked to him on the phone yesterday, I called him George rather than Mr. Vice-President. But, in public, it's Mr. Vice-President, because that's who he is.
>
> Dan Quayle

I didn't like it and I didn't inhale it.

President Bill Clinton, skirting the question of him having smoked marijuana when he was a student

It's no exaggeration to say that the undecideds could go one way or another.

George H. W. Bush, at a campaign rally, October 1988

> **Ronald Reagan, in 1982**

Now we are trying to get unemployment to go up, and I think we are going to succeed.

You cannot be President of the United States if you don't have faith. Remember Lincoln, going to his knees in times of trial and the Civil War and all that stuff. You can't be. And we are blessed. So don't feel sorry for—don't cry for me, Argentina.

George H.W. Bush

Charles de Gaulle, former French President

China is a big country, inhabited by many Chinese.

Add one little bit on the end ... Think of "potatoe," how's it spelled? You're right phonetically, but what else? There ya go ... all right!
Vice-President Dan Quayle "correcting" a student's (correct) spelling of the word "potato" during a spelling bee at an elementary school in the Luis Munoz Rivera School in Trenton, New Jersey

You know, if I were a single man, I might ask that mummy out. That's a good-looking mummy.
President Bill Clinton, appraising "Juanita," a newly-discovered Inca mummy on display at the National Geographic Museum

If two wrongs don't make a right, try three.

Richard Nixon

The United States has much to offer the third world war.

Ronald Reagan, in 1975 (meaning the Third World); he made the same mistake several times

Facts are stupid things.

Ronald Reagan, addressing the Republican National Convention in 1988. He was misquoting John Adams who, in 1778, wrote, "Facts are stubborn things." Reagan repeated the mistake several times

Justice is incidental to law and order.

J. Edgar Hoover, former FBI Director

A zebra does not change its spots.

Al Gore, attacking President Bush in 1992

Dan Quayle, 1990

For NASA, space is still a high priority.

I didn't go down there with any plan for the Americas, or anything. I went down to find out from them and (learn) their views. You'd be surprised. They're all individual countries.

Ronald Reagan, in 1982, explaining how his five-day Latin American trip had changed his outlook on the region

President Richard Nixon

I'm glad I'm not Brezhnev. Being the Russian leader in the Kremlin, you never know if someone's tape-recording what you say.

Waste of time. They're all just a load of balladonnas.

Lord Blyton (1899–1987), English politican (he meant, "primadonnas")

I should have caught the mistake on that spelling bee card. But as Mark Twain once said, "You should never trust a man who has only one way to spell a word."
Vice-President Dan Quayle, actually quoting from President Andrew Jackson

I was provided with additional input that was radically different from the truth. I assisted in furthering that version.
Colonel Oliver North, from his testimony during the Iran–Contra scandal

It could have been spinach dip or something.

Monica Lewinsky, on the famous stain on her dress

You mean there are two Koreas?

Richard Kneip, US Ambassador Designate to Singapore, upon being asked his opinion of the North–South Korean divide during congressional hearings

We are not without accomplishment. We have managed to distribute poverty equally.
Nguyen Co Thatch, ex-Foreign Minister of Vietnam

Harry S. Truman, former US President

Always be sincere, even if you don't mean it.

I am not a chauvinist, obviously . . . I believe in women's rights for every woman but my own.
Harold Washington, Chicago Mayor

Things are more like they are now than they ever were before.
Dwight D. Eisenhower, former US President

Don't believe any false rumors unless you hear them from me.

New Orleans Mayor Vic Schiro, uttering arguably his all-time greatest malapropism while inspecting damage resulting from Hurricane Betsy

That's the way the cookie bounces.

Vic Schiro, New Orleans Mayor—famous for his malapropisms, called "Schiroisms"

The single most important two things we can do . . .

Tony Blair

Outside of the killings, (Washington) has one of the lowest crime rates in the country.

Marion Barry, Mayor of Washington DC

What's a man got to do to get in the top fifty?

President Bill Clinton, reacting to a survey of journalists that ranked the Lewinsky scandal as the 53rd most significant story of the century

My fellow Americans. I'm pleased to tell you today that I've signed legislation that will outlaw Russia forever. (Laughter.) We begin bombing in five minutes. (Laughter.)

Ronald Reagan, during a 1984 press conference about negotiations with Russia over nuclear arms reduction, in what he thought was a sound check for the radio engineers. The Russian ambassador was sitting nearby

Lydon B. Johnson, US President, 1964

We are not going to send American boys nine or ten thousand miles to do what Asian boys ought to be doing for themselves.

It's like an Alcatraz around my neck.
Thomas M. Menino, Boston Mayor, on the shortage of parking spaces in his city. He meant albatross, of course

Every prime minister needs a Willie.

Margaret Thatcher, referring to Lord William Whitelaw

We're going to have the best-educated American people in the world. Dan Quayle, September 1988

No woman in my time will be Prime Minister or Chancellor or Foreign Secretary—not the top jobs. Anyway, I wouldn't want to be Prime Minister. You have to give yourself one hundred percent.

Margaret Thatcher, interviewed in the *Sunday Telegraph* in October 1969, when she was Shadow Spokesman on Education

Wait a minute! I'm not interested in agriculture. I want the military stuff.
Senator William Scott, during a briefing in which officials began telling him about missile silos

The Internet is a great way to get on the Net.
Bob Dole, Republican presidential candiate

Ronald Reagan

There is a mandate to impose a voluntary return to traditional values.

Only one thing would be worse than the status quo. And that would be for the status quo to become the norm.
Elizabeth Dole in 1999, during a campaign speech

It isn't pollution that's harming the environment. It's the impurities in our air and water that are doing it.
Dan Quayle

The streets are safe in Philadelphia—it's only the people who make them unsafe.
Frank Rizzo, ex-Police Chief and Mayor of Philadelphia

152

> To you, and to the people you represent, the great people of the government of Israel . . . Egypt, excuse me.
>
> President Gerald R. Ford, proposing a toast at a state dinner held in his honor by the Egyptian leader, Anwar el-Sadat, December 1975

One word sums up probably the responsibility of any Vice-President, and that one word is "to be prepared."
Dan Quayle, 1989

I do not like this word bomb. It is not a bomb. It is a device which is exploding.
Jacques Le Blanc, French Ambassador to New Zealand describing France's nuclear testing in 1995

Doesn't the fight for survival also justify swindle and theft? In self-defense, anything goes.
Imelda Marcos, former First Lady of the Philippines

I have had great financial sex.
Ross Perot in a speech; he was aiming to say "I have had great financial success"

CUSTOMER SERVICE

**DO NOT use massage chair without clothing...
and NEVER force any body part into the
backrest area while the rollers are moving.**
Warning note on massage chair

**The wines at
our hotel shall
leave you
nothing to
hope for.**
Notice in a
European hotel

**People can have (the Model T
in) any color . . . so long
as it's black.**
Henry Ford, founder of the Ford
Motor Company. The company was
forced to move with the times,
introducing a choice of colors in
1925. Though from 1909 the range
had a singular look to it

Do not look into laser with remaining eye.
Warning notice on a laser-pointer device

Mushrooms cultivated on substrate
from extensive agriculture which is
permitted in organic farming during
a transitional period.
A label on a packet of mushrooms sold in
upmarket supermarket chain Waitrose

This is a message for all passengers in the fourth carriage: can you please teach the gentleman who keeps trying to open the doors exactly how they close, preferably by holding him firmly and letting them close repeatedly on his head.
Announcement by driver of a London Underground train

This is your captain speaking. Is there anyone aboard who can lend me 80 dollars?
Unnamed pilot of a chartered British holiday jet on its way to Malaga, in Spain, which was forced to make an emergency landing in Morocco after running low on fuel. Finding himself $80 short, he was obliged to ask to pass the hat to the 166 passengers onboard

Hens kept in batteries are better cared for . . .
Ed Oakley on McDonald's UK's policy of buying eggs from battery-farmed hens

Aer Lingus spokesperson

What we are doing is in the interest of everybody, bar possibly the consumer.

Not dishwasher safe
Warning label on TV remote control

Do not dangle the mouse
by its cable or throw the
mouse at co-workers.
Handy instruction in a user's manual
for an SGI computer

**This product is
not to be used
in bathrooms.**
Warning notice on
a bathroom heater
manufactured by
Holmes Co.

**Caution: Cape
does not enable
user to fly.**
Warning notice on the
Batman costume made
by Kenner Products

And
the next train arriving on
platform four is the Dunblane
train. This train is very overcrowded,
so if there are any passengers standing
in the doorways, just throw them out
the way.
**Tannoy announcement at Haymarket
station, Edinburgh**

Don't Kill Your Wife with Work.
Let Electricity Do it!
London Electricity poster

Caution: The contents of this bottle should not be fed to fish.
Warning label on a bottle of dog shampoo

Do not drive with sunshield in place.
Warning label on cardboard sun reflector

The cup holder in my PC is broken and I am within my warranty period. How do I go about getting that fixed?
Caller contacting technical support at Novell NetWire SysOp.

Remove child before folding.
Advisory note on a child's stroller

I am sorry for the delay to this service. This is due to signal problems. And if you look out to the right-hand side of the train, you will see the Wembley signal control room. I've just asked them on the radio to look at this train, so if you would all like to show them exactly what you think of them, please go ahead. One or two fingers should be all you need.
Helpful advice from the driver of a London Underground train, on a stretch of line that was overground

Unfortunately for you lot, we are now stuck behind a broken-down train. We'll be here for quite a while. But I don't care: I'm now on overtime.

Announcement by driver of a London Underground train

Caution: blade is extremely sharp. Keep out of children.

Warning on knife blade manufactured by Olfa Corporation

Do not attempt to stop the blade with your hand.

Warning label on chainsaw

Product will be hot after heating

Notice on Marks and Spencer Bread and Butter pudding

This is a customer announcement. Would the nut-case who just jumped onto the track please get back onto the platform as the rats get jealous when someone invades their territory.

Announcement by London Underground